ANCIENT COIN COLLECTING V

The Romaion / Byzantine Culture

WAYNE G. SAYLES

Published by

 **krause
publications**

700 E. State Street
Iola, WI 54990-0001
Telephone: 715/445-2214

Please call or write for our free catalog. Our toll-free number to place
an order or obtain a free catalog is 800-258-0929 or please use our
regular business telephone 715-445-2214 for editorial comment and
further information.

Library of Congress Catalog Number: 95-82428
ISBN: 0-87341-637-6

Printed in the United States of America

Byz´•an•tine:
   b. Highly complicated; intricate and involved...
                  (American Heritage Dictionary)

This book is dedicated to
Betty J. Sayles
who must at times have thought her son's life byzantine

PREFACE

One would think that choosing a book's title would be the easiest part of writing it, but not so in this case. After embracing the term *Romaion* in Volume one of this series, we encountered some minor resistance to the expression. It is, after all, a change from the norm. One critic was already thinking ahead, wondering what the title of Volume V would be? On the other hand, we also received encouragement from numismatists, whose opinions we value. We will not reiterate the argument here, but the essence of our position is that the term *Byzantine* is inaccurate and inappropriate. The reason that we have brought this polemic to the doorstep of our readers is neither to grind an axe, nor lead a crusade. It is simply to make a new generation of collectors aware that there is an alternative view.

One criticism which we took to heart was that beginning collectors who were unfamiliar with either or both of these terms could be confused. We have therefore made a concerted effort to keep the reader aware that both terms are used—and usable. Hence the rather ambiguous title for this volume. We are not alone in the desire to find a more acceptable term than Byzantine. The titles of Harlan Berk's , *Eastern Roman Successors of the Sestertius* and *Roman Gold Coins of the Medieval World 383-1453 AD,* suggest that he too had some reservations about the name Byzantine. Dr. John Lhotka titled his book *Introduction to East Roman (Byzantine) Coinage.* In *The Fall of the Roman Empire: A Reappraisal,* Michael Grant identifies Justinian I as an "East Roman (Byzantine) Emperor". The parenthetical "Byzantine" is his. There are many others, including some historians of renown, who have indicated through the titles of their published works that the term "Byzantine" is not universally favored. Nevertheless, the world of academia— often intractable in such matters—will be slow to accept any change. This is not too surprising, nor is it necessarily a bad thing. However, we believe that change is in order, and we are only doing our small part here to help make that evident.

The arrangement of this volume is identical to its predecessors. That is, there are many short sections compiled in a loose framework of "chapters". These sections approach various subjects of general interest to the beginner—for whom this book is written. None of them constitute a comprehensive discussion of the topic. After all, this is a road map to the hobby of collecting, not a thesis or dissertation. They simply introduce the reader to various aspects of the coinage and its artistic or historical associations. These vignettes are meant to stand alone as the reader digests one or more sections at a time. While most books are meant to be read from cover to cover in one passing. The books in this series differ intentionally. They are meant to offer information in short "bytes" rather than as flowing discourse. Consequently, there will be some minor repetitive detail—although not enough to become tedious we would hope.

Even the experienced collector should benefit from the many illustrations of superior coins herein, and perhaps from the observations of a different set of eyes. We have tried to be as accurate as literature and research at our disposal will allow, but inevitably there will be new discoveries and interpretations that we have missed. For that, we apologize in advance. In this field, as in all fields of numismatics, there is a substantial amount of research being undertaken by professionals and amateurs alike. Serious students and collectors would be well advised to subscribe to the scholarly journals which announce this work and publish the results.

Romaion or Byzantine coins constitute one of the most exciting fields available to the collector of modest means. Even the great rarities in this series do not command the prices that a mediocre scarcity realizes in the field of Greek or Roman coinage. The most expensive of these coins are measured in thousands of dollars, while the most expensive Greek coins are measured in hundreds of thousands of dollars. The least expensive may be purchased for less than the cost of lunch at a fast-food restaurant. If ancient coins on the whole are under appreciated and undervalued, then "Byzantine" coins are greatly undervalued. Not everyone will be attracted to these coins. They offer a certain charm, but they are not visibly impressive—for the most part. Their attraction lies more so in the mystery that is associated with their history and origin.

It is still possible in this series for the ardent collector to find rare and even unique coins in dealer junk boxes. In fact, one has a much greater chance of finding a unique bronze from the Carthage, Thessalonica or Trebizond mint than a key date Indian Head penny. The reason is simple. Few collectors or dealers are sufficiently aware of the rarities. That is not at all surprising, given the nature of the coinage. While rarities *do* abound, and they *are* cheap, one really has to know the coins to cash in on that fact. Like any other category of coins from the ancient world, these need to be approached with a specific methodology. It is tempting to take a shotgun approach and collect a little of this and a little of that, but seldom does this approach bring real satisfaction or a meaningful collection. Concentration and focus are the keys to success. It is best to choose a relatively narrow field of interest and then expand it as time goes on. Starting out with a loosely defined objective is a sure recipe for wasted time and money.

There are many possible approaches to building a collection. One could, for example, concentrate on coins from a particular mint or imperial dynasty. Another approach might be to assemble a type set of coins depicting saints or angels. An ambitious project might include assembling a date set for one of the longer reigning emperors. If one has a preference for historical time capsules, there are many coins that can be tied to a military adventure or political event. The possibilities are nearly endless.

Where does one start? Well that depends on personal interests, but the answer is "anywhere". Pick up a coin—any coin— and learn what its place in history is. Find out what the world was like when that coin was struck. Learn what makes that particular coin different from all the others that lie in trays and boxes here and there. Also, learn what coins are related to that specimen and belong by its side. This is when the collecting begins. A search for specific coins that answer preconceived questions or expand one's awareness of a series is a labor of love and joy.

Having spent the better part of 32 years studying ancient Greek and Roman coins, it has been a distinct pleasure to compile the information presented here. We have been inspired to look at coinage of this time and place in a framework which we had not previously considered. The history represented by these coins is fascinating, and it is a challenge to capture the essence of a complicated personality or reign in a few paragraphs of text. We have tried throughout to present information that will inspire the reader to seek additional sources. Anticipating that in some cases we might succeed, we have presented a rather extensive bibliography. It is our hope that, in distilling some of the information available, we will serve as a catalyst for others to delve deeper into the mysteries of Romaion / Byzantine coinage.

Gainesville, Missouri 1998   W.G.S.

ACKNOWLEDGMENTS

We are indebted to Peter Lampinen, friend and dedicated numismatist, for sharing his expertise on the imitations of "Byzantine" coinage. This is a very broad subject, on which information is obscure and too little is published. We are very fortunate to benefit from his many years of study and professional work in the field. The kind permission of Professor Clifton Fox to quote from his *Celator* article—which includes information about the origin and meaning of the title *Basileus*—is gratefully acknowledged. We also thank noted Byzantinist Simon Bendall for permission to include extracts and illustrations from his articles in *The Celator.* Our thanks as well to Chris Connell for sharing with us the abstraction of Christ's portrait on coins of John VIII. The special font for reproduction of epigraphical titles in the Gallery of Emperors and Empresses was provided by Dan Clark.

Since this book is, like those before it, a synthesis of information from many sources, it is not possible to acknowledge all of the numismatists who have made a contribution. The scholarship in this field is truly astounding, and a cursory glance at the bibliographies will reveal the names of those who lead in this respect. Let us reiterate our thanks to everyone who has taken the time and made the effort to share their knowledge in print. If we may single out just one, there can be little doubt that David R. Sear has done more to foster new collector interest in this series than all other authors combined. His *Byzantine Coins and Their Values* is indispensable for the beginner and expert alike.

Illustrated in this fifth volume of the *Ancient Coin Collecting* series are a great many superb specimens, including some of exceptional rarity. We are deeply indebted to Classical Numismatic Group, of Lancaster, Pennsylvania; Harlan J. Berk, of Chicago, Illinois; Leu Numismatik of Zürich, Switzerland; M&M Numismatics Ltd. of Basel, Switzerland, Frank L. Kovacs of San Mateo, California and Edward J. Waddell of Gaithersburg, Maryland for permission to reproduce photos from monographs, fixed price lists and auction catalogues issued by their firms.

As this project moves into its final phase I must acknowledge, more so than ever, the invaluable assistance provided by my wife and companion Doris—who through her vigilance and forbearance keeps it all together.

TABLE OF CONTENTS

The city of Byzantion, virtually in the back yard of Alexander's Macedon and at the crossroads of post Alexandrine power struggles, was nevertheless a place of little consequence in the pre-Roman era. The city was named for Byzas, its mythical founder, who was according to legend a son of Poseidon and Ceroëssa (daughter of Io).

Throughout most of its early history, the city basked in a milieu of tranquil prosperity and managed not to attract the attention of ambitious leaders or military strategists. It enjoyed the good providence of a deep water harbor and superior protection from storms. In the war between Rome and Macedon, Byzantion supported the former. With their victory, the city acquired both the protection of Rome and the endowment of important commercial privileges.

The city of Constantinople being presented to Christ by Constantine the Great (Mosaic over the south door of Hagia Sophia, dated to the late 10th century)

During the civil war between Septimius Severus and Pescennius Niger, Byzantion unfortunately aligned with Niger and was completely devastated in that losing cause. Although Severus rebuilt the city, it was not to fully recover for another century. The geographical advantages of Byzantion were clearly recognized by Constantine the Great—who had consolidated power in the Roman world like no single emperor since Augustus. Seeking to distance himself from the decadence and political intrigues of Rome, he set upon the construction of a magnificent capital at this site. The new city was named Constantinople and raised to a rank equal with Rome itself. It was a spectacle above all others. The great imperial palace of Constantine and his successors was filled with wonders and wealth like no other before or since. This palace—consisting of many residences, churches and pavilions—covered the whole length of the Hippodrome, and extended from the main church, Hagia Sophia (Holy Wisdom), to the sea. , Recent discoveries of palace remains are just now undergoing archaeological excavation.

Constantinople became the jewel of the East and the new bastion of Roman culture—surviving for more than a thousand years after

1

Constantine's death. Its unique place in history could not have been foreseen by its founder, but the visions of Constantine, both at the Milvian Bridge and on the shore of the Bosphorus, left a momentous imprint on western civilization. The culture which developed at this city was remarkable in many ways. In the past half-century, historians have begun to revise their opinion of the "Byzantines" from a society of opulence and decadence to one of scientific and cultural achievement. The 12th century Renaissance of the Romaioi in Constantinople and Asia Minor is now recognized as a precursor to that of the Italians some two centuries later.

In contrast to the sculptural idealism of Classical Greek coinage, and the stark verism of Roman numismatic art, the coins of the Eastern Roman emperors are often crude and emotionless. For this reason, they were looked down upon by the collecting community for centuries. Only in recent decades have the images been recognized as spiritual abstractions rather than examples of inept draftsmanship. There were three distinct elements of the Romaion culture: first were the Greek influences and traditions, stemming from the indigenous population and the physical location of the cultural center; secondly, the administrative organization of the Romans added a layer of official language and imperial iconography; and finally, the rise of Christianity as the dominant religion was reflected in expressions of faith in art and literature. All of these elements may be seen in the coinage of these people.

The imperial titles found on these coins were derived partly from those of Hellenistic kings. Also, the numerals representing denomination and officina were usually expressed in the Greek system. Iconographic details, like the diadem and various garments, are reflective of Greek influence as well.

The system of mints and denominations was based on the Roman model. Dates on Romaion/Byzantine coinage were often expressed in Roman numerals rather than Greek letter-numerals. In the early days of the eastern empire, standard Roman imagery prevailed. For example, portraits were often presented in profile, personifications were commonplace, and standard consular imagery was retained.

Over time, the imagery became increasingly religious, and Roman iconographic details evolved into Christian imagery. Nike, for example, was transformed into an angel. The globe, a standard Roman symbol of authority and dominion, was readily transformed into a Christian image by addition of a cross above. The result, called a *globus cruciger*, represented the dual role of the emperor as head of the state and the church. The nimbus (aureole or halo) was a celestial reference that also stems from Roman imagery. It was used symbolically by Roman emperors, even before the adoption of Christianity as a state religion. A portrait of Christ first appears on the coinage of Justinian II (AD 685-

2

695). But strangely enough, during the period known as the Iconoclasm, religious images were banned entirely for a time. Later coinage, in contrast, is almost exclusively religious in imagery.

The merging of these three main influences formed a distinctive culture which left its mark on history and also left behind a prolific coinage for us to study and enjoy. From our perspective, it is neither Greek, nor Roman. They called themselves the Romaioi—the Greek word for Romans. Later historians have labeled them Byzantine, ostensibly after the name of the site before its refounding in AD 330.

AV hyperpyron of Andronicus II (Virgin within the walls of Constantinople)

As with all great cultures before it, the empire that was ruled from Constantinople finally collapsed. It withstood the ravages of many would-be conquerors, but each in turn took its toll. Finally, in 1453, the means to resist were no longer sufficient. The city succumbed to the onslaught of the Turks and the last *Basileus Romaion* bravely fell in combat on its crumbling walls.

Today, we find that Byzantine Studies has become a main thread of academia. It is itself a major discipline. International conferences are convened each year to share new discoveries and exchange information— much of which comes from the study of coinage surviving this great empire's tenure.

The Hippodrome at Constantinople after the Islamic conquest

3

IVSTINIANVS
(Justinian)

DN =
Dominus
Noster

PP =
Perpetuus

AVC=
Augustus

"Our Lord, Justinian, forever, Augustus"

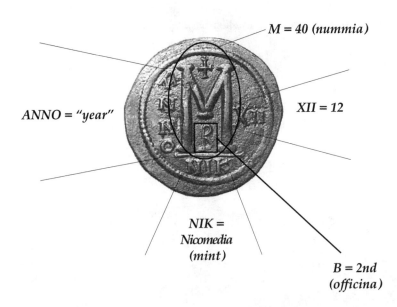

M = 40 (nummia)

ANNO = "year"

XII = 12

NIK =
Nicomedia
(mint)

B = 2nd
(officina)

Justinian I, AD 527-565. AE Follis (40 nummia). 23.27 gm. Year 12 (AD 538/9). Nicomedia mint, Officina B. Obv: Helmeted and cuirassed bust facing, shield over left shoulder, globus cruciger in upraised right hand. Cross in field to right. Rev: Large M, ANNO to left, XII to right. Cross above. B/NIK above and below exergual line. (Depicted actual size.)

Mints

It is not always a simple matter of reading the mint mark on a coin of this series to determine where it was struck. Although many do not have such marks, others use only obscure symbols and some actually use the designators of another mint altogether. To identify the mint, it is sometimes necessary to examine very minute details and make very close comparisons to provenanced pieces. Fortunately, there are also a great many coins which do bear recognizable marks. The more common mints are listed below for your quick reference. In many cases, we know that a mint existed in a general region—especially in Spain, Italy, or North Africa—but we do not know its precise name or location. At certain mints the issue was brief, usually due to political or economic urgency.

List of Mintmarks		Officinas
Alexandretta¹	*ΑΛΕΧΑΝΔ*	*A= 1*
Alexandria	*ΑΛΕξ, ΑΛΕΙ*	*B= 2*
Antioch²	*AN, ANTX, ANTIX*	*Γ= 3*
Carthage	*CAR, CRT, CT, KAR,*	*Δ= 4*
	KART. KRT	*Є = 5*
Catania	*CAT*	*S= 6*
Cherson	*XEPCШNOC, ⳁ, ⳁX*	*Z= 7*
Constantinople	*CON, CONOB*	*H= 8*
Cyprus³	*CΠP, KVΠP, KVΠP୪*	*Θ= 9*
Cyzicus	*KY, KYZ*	*I = 10*
Isaura⁴	*ISAYR*	
Jerusalem	*IЄPOCO*	
Naples	*NЄ*	
Nicomedia	*NI, NIC, NIK, NIKOM*	
Ravenna	*RA, RAB, RAV*	
Rome	*ROM, ROMOB*	
Sardinia	*S*	
Seleucia⁵	*SЄL, SЄLISЧ, ꙅЄLIꙅЧ*	
Syracuse	*SCL, SECILIA*	
Theoupolis	*ThEЧP, ϴS, ϴYΠOΛS*	
Thessalonica	*TES, TESOB, ϴEC, ϴES*	

¹ *Modern Iskenderun, Turkey*
² *Antioch renamed Theoupolis in AD 528*
³ *Mints at Constantia and Nicosia*
⁴ *In Isauria (modern Turkey)*
⁵ *In Cilicia (modern Turkey)*

Note: Several additional cities briefly struck, or are conjectured to have struck, coins during this period. Among them are Arta, Carthagena, Constantine, Magnesia, Nicaea, Perugia, Philippopolis and Salona.

Denominations

Gold denominations were relatively stable throughout the early period, with the *solidus* (72 to the pound) being the standard. This coin was originally introduced by Constantine the Great. The aureus (60 to the pound) was still struck during the reigns of Anastasius and Justinian, but few examples survive. A full weight solidus of pure gold (*obryzum*) weighed 24 carats. The designation for pure gold (OB) became part of the exergual legend, e.g. CONOB for pure gold struck at Constantinople. Starting during the reign of Justinian, and continuing into the eighth century, lightweight solidi were also struck with values ranging between 20 and 23 siliquae. That is, 20 to 23 carats (1 siliqua = 1 carat). Some were marked to indicate their value (for example, XXOB for 20 carats). The reason for their weight difference is unknown, but presumably it was prompted by some external necessity. Gold fractional denominations included the *semissis* and *tremissis*—1/2 and 1/3 solidus respectively. The 1/2 tremissis, a rare denomination equal to the silver *hexagram*, was issued under several emperors but from its scarcity seems not to have enjoyed much popularity—perhaps due to its very small size and fragile thin flan. Gold and silver multiples exist in this series but are extremely rare, and were obviously not produced for widespread circulation. Few collectors will ever see, much less own, coins of these multiple denominations. Therefore, we have chosen not to include them in our tables of denominations. Specialized studies and catalogues should be consulted for information about these exceptional issues.

Marks of Value	
M = 40	Є or Ч = 5
ΛΓ = 33	Δ = 4
Λ = 30	Γ = 3
K = 20	B = 2
IS = 16	A = 1
IB = 12	XXXX=40
I = 10	XXX=30
H = 8	XX =20
S = 6	X =10

A later form of the solidus, with thinner and broader flan is known as the *histamenon nomisma*. About AD 1000, the gold coins became cup-shaped and were known as *trachy*. Numismatists today refer to them (perhaps inaccurately) as *scyphate*. Denominationally, they are still referred to as the histamenon whether flat or "scyphate". Early issues were struck in gold of relatively high purity, but the series became heavily debased in later years. Eventually, they degenerated into silver or

Denominational relationships*	
AV solidus =	7,200
AV semissis =	3,600
AV tremissis =	2,400
AR hexagram =	1,200
AR miliarense =	600
AR siliqua =	300
AR 1/2 siliqua =	150
AE follis =	40
AE nummus =	1

ca. 800 AD. Relationships varied greatly depending on the period of issue.

billon coins and are referred to as aspron trachy, AR (silver) trachy or billon trachy depending on their composition. The old solidus continued to be issued, but was reduced in weight and redesignated the tetarteron. In the 10th century the histamenon and tetarteron fell dramatically in fineness. Alexius I (1081-1118) completely revised the monetary system and introduced the *hyperpyron* (meaning "highly refined", which was a coin of about 20 carat gold. This did not last for long, as the gold was progressively debased until it too became an electrum coin of very low purity. The debasement was so severe that the color of the coin turned to a very pale yellow—almost white. Hence, the term *aspron* (white) trachy.

Silver coinage is relatively scarce throughout the series, yet is not very widely collected. Therefore, the prices of silver issues do not generally reflect their rarity. The reason for this would seem to be that gold is actually plentiful and a collector can often purchase a gold coin of a relatively common ruler for the same price as a silver coin—often for less. This tends to hold silver coin prices at lower levels than one might normally expect. During the seventh century and earlier, the main silver coins were the *siliqua* and its fractions—as well as the hexagram, which was equal to four siliquae. Later, the main silver coin was the *miliaresion* (earlier called miliarense). Although this denomination was first struck during the reign of Constantine the Great (AD 307-337), it was a relatively rare denomination until the mid 8th century when Constantine V issued a new standard type with a cross on three steps. Constantine IX introduced the 2/3 miliaresion, which was continued until the Alexian reform of 1092. At that time, the miliaresion was replaced by an electrum trachy. In the 13th century, a smaller flat silver coin modeled on contemporary Venetian coinage was introduced. It was known as the *basilikon*. In a more debased form it is known as the *asper*. Finally, during the reign of John V, the *stavraton* was introduced. This relatively large silver coin, characterized by its very stylized images, stayed in circulation until the fall of Constantinople. It was also issued in fractional denominations.

Anastasius restored the large bronze coin as a circulating denomination under his monetary reform of AD 498. At the same time, the denominational mark, e.g. M (Greek letter/numeral = 40) was incorporated into the reverse design. The large bronze had been struck, at least in the west, during the reign of Zeno but was not widely circulated. This issue is normally referred to as the *follis*. In this survey, we shall refer to it by the denomination 40 nummi whenever that mark may be found on the coin itself, and by the term follis when there are not any denominational marks. Likewise, smaller denominations without specific marks of value will be referred to as 1/2 follis etc. as best determined from the coin's size and weight. Under Maurice Tiberius, the Cherson mint produced a bronze coin denominated 8 *pentanummia* (=40 nummi or 1 follis) and a 4 pentanummia coin (=20 nummi or 1/2 follis). These issues are marked on the reverse by the Greek numerals H (8) and Δ (4). The pentanummia is equal to 5 nummi, therefore, 8 pentanummia = 40 nummi.

Justinian II, AE quartered follis
Constantinople mint, year 3

In the 7th century, production of bronze coins reached a low point when massive quantities of folles were restruck over earlier types. The dies created for these coins were crude to begin with, but then the planchet preparation and striking was even worse. As a result, we see many coins from the time of Heraclius through Justinian II which look extremely crude. The larger folles of earlier reigns were some-times quartered, and then restruck. In other cases, planchets were roughly cut out of hammered sheets of bronze. Therefore, we find a great many irregular shaped coins from this period. Under the Alexian reform the follis was replaced by the bronze *tetarteron*—which under Andronicus II was redesignated the *assarion*. Also, some of the later scyphate coins which were technically billon or silver had so little precious metal that we refer to them as AE trachy.

New discoveries are frequent in this series and very common coins can yield important historical information. Also, the coins as a whole have not received the kind of scrutiny and interest that the Greek and Roman series has. New denominations, new mints and even new rulers have surfaced in the past decade and there are many discoveries yet to be made amongst the most inconspicuous of coins residing in a collection or dealer's junk box. For example, finding a tiny bronze with the letter Gamma or Delta on the reverse can be an extraordinary catch. These are rare denomi-nations (3 and 4 nummi) which are unknown for many mints and reigns. Yours may well be a discovery piece.

Having said this, we must admit that the discoveries are still there to be made because it is not an easy field to master. The coins are hard to see, harder to read, usually crude and/or corroded and sometimes impossible to interpret. It takes a lot of practice and a sharp eye—but no other field of ancient coinage offers greater potential reward for the effort expended.

Major Denominations in Gold

AV 1/2 tremissis

AV solidus

AV tremissis

AV tetarteron

AV semissis

AV histamenon nomisma

EL aspron trachy

AV hyperpyron

Major Denominations in Silver

120 nummi

hexagram

250 nummi

basilikon

1/2 siliqua

billon tornese

siliqua

1/8 stavraton

2/3 miliaresion
(400 nummi)

1/2 stavraton

miliaresion

trachy

stavraton

Major Denominations in Bronze

nummus *2 nummi* *3 nummi* *4 nummi* *5 nummi*
pentanummium

6 nummi *8 nummi* *10 nummi* *12 nummi* *16 nummi*
decanummium

4 pentanummia *20 nummi (1/2 follis)* *30 nummi (3/4 follis)*
(20 nummi)

33 nummi *8 pentanummia* *40 nummi (follis)*
(40 nummi)

tetarteron *5 nummi* *10 nummi* *20 nummi*

30 nummi *40 nummi*

Dates

The dating of coins in this series is sporadic, and mostly limited to the early period. Two methods of dating were used. The first, and most common, reflected the regnal date of the emperor. That is, the date in years from his accession. Some emperors who ruled as co-emperor prior to their sole reign started counting regnal dates from their first accession. The regnal dates sometimes got to be fairly large. For example, Justinian's regnal dates reached 39, and Heraclius' 31. Constantine VII could have reached 51—but dates had, with a few exceptions, been abandoned on coinage by the time of his reign.

The second method of dating was to use indictional years. The indiction was a fifteen year cycle in which taxes were levied and adjusted. As a rule, regnal dates were preceded by the word ANNO, while indictional dates were preceded by the letter IN or IND. However, as Grierson points out, there are exceptions where the word anno is used inappropriately with an indiction date and sometimes numerals appear alone without any indication of the system used. To calculate the AD date from an indictional reference, one must know which year of the indiction was in effect at the time of the emperor's accession. This is accomplished by using a chart, or calculating the years from the first indiction which started on September 1, AD 312. For those emperors who reigned more than 15 years it is possible to have an identical indictional date on two coins struck 15 years apart. From this it is easy to see how dating often requires more than a simple reading of the coin's legends. In the chart below, as an example, are the regnal and indictional dates for the emperor Justin II who was crowned in the 14th indiction.

Regnal and Indictional Dates for Justin II		
AD DATE	REGNAL YEAR	INDICTION YEAR
565/66	1	14
566/67	2	15
567/68	3	1
568/69	4	2
569/70	5	3
570/71	6	4
571/72	7	5
572/73	8	6
573/74	9	7
574/75	10	8
575/76	11	9
576/77	12	10
577/78	13	11

The Scyphate Coinage

Constantine IX, AD 1042-1055
AV histamenon nomisma (x1.5)

Manuel I, AD 1143-1180
EL aspron trachy

The term scyphate or *nummi scyphati* seems actually to be of 19th century derivation. It is taken to mean "cup shaped" and is used to describe those unusual coins with concave and convex surfaces which are among the most enigmatic of the entire series. There have been all sorts of hypotheses about the motivation for striking coins in this shape, but none of them quite satisfy the question. There are no primary sources which explain the nature of these coins. The etymology of the term is convoluted, but it will suffice to say that it is a misnomer. For a thorough discussion, see the article by P. Grierson listed in the bibliography on page 15. Be that as it may, the term is still used universally. We may do well to discard the term scyphate, as Professor Grierson suggests, but then we should also discard the equally inappropriate term "Byzantine". In all practicality, neither term is likely to disappear in the near future—misnomer or not. If we do not know *why* these coins were made, we do at least know *how*. Simon Bendall and David Sellwood have shown that the process is one of "double striking". To explain more fully, the following is essay extracted, with permission, from Bendall's article which appeared in *The Celator*, June 1998.

The double striking of late Byzantine scyphate coins
by Simon Bendall

The reason for making scyphate coins is obscure. What is certain is that their manufacture would have been much harder than the production of a flat coin. In order to produce a well struck scyphate it is necessary that both obverse and reverse dies should have the same radius of curvature in order to mate exactly. This seems to have been beyond Byzantine engineering skills, at least when the scyphate coins ceased to be very shallow and especially since hundreds of interchangeable dies were in use at the same time. It might have been possible to mate one pair of dies but not to make every one of several hundred obverse dies compatible with every reverse die.

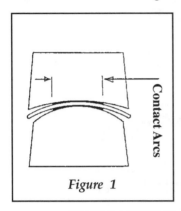

Figure 1

We can see from figure 1 that if the obverse, or upper, die was shallower than the lower, a vertical blow would only strike up the detail in the centre of the flan.

On the other hand, figure 2 shows that if the lower die was shallower than the upper, then only the edge of the blank would receive an impression of the design. No coins exist that lack the centre of the design but there are many which lack the edges, including the legends. Thus it appears that the mint authorities made sure that all obverse dies had a larger radius than the lower dies. The problem remained that the part of the design on the edges of both sides of the coin were not struck up and this of course would include the emperor's name and title.

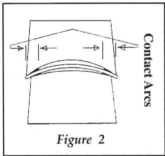

Figure 2

If, however, the coin was struck twice with the upper die rocked slightly from side to side a fuller impression would result (figure 3). Rocking the upper die without lifting it from the lower die would no doubt have been possible when the curvature of the coins was quite shallow. It seems that by the beginning of the twelfth century, if not earlier, in striking the upper die was occa-

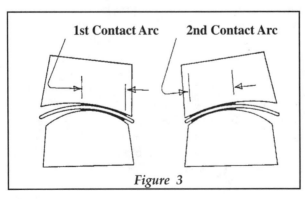

1st Contact Arc   **2nd Contact Arc**

Figure 3

sionally lifted from the flan between blows, especially at the mint of Thessalonica. There, even as early as the reign of Alexius I (1081-1118), the curvature of the gold coins was deeper than on the Constantinopolitan issues. This, of course, produces very typical evidence of double striking.

It is obvious that, at least from the mid-twelfth century, even at Constantinople, the obverse die was not usually rocked but lifted between blows. The lifting results in some displacement, either linear or rotational or perhaps both and this is in fact what we commonly see. There is also evidence that scyphate coins were not just struck by two blows with a single die but that two obverse dies were often used. These would have been held by two mint workers since it is impossible to believe that after one blow the man holding the upper die would put it down and pick up another one!

The use of two upper dies can, however, only be identified when each die was of a slightly different design. Figure 4 shows this clearly. The coin is a silver trachy of John III of Nicaea (1222-1254); the die used to strike the left hand side depicts the youthful Christ with a nimbus containing single pellets enclosed between double lines while the right hand die had a nimbus with five pellets enclosed between an upper double line and a lower single line. There is no possibility that the engraver had made an error by engraving a single pellet on the left side of the die and five pellets on the right side of the same die since both sides of the left die are clearly showing a single pellet on both sides.

Figure 4 (x2)

Bibliography — Scyphates

Bendall, Simon. "The double striking of late Byzantine scyphate coins", *The Celator,* 12:06, June 1998, pp. 20ff.

Bendall, Simon and David Sellwood. "The method of striking scyphate coins using two obverse dies in light of an early thirteenth century hoard", *Numismatic Chronicle,* 1978, pp. 93-115.

Grierson, P. "Nummi scyphati. The story of a misunderstanding", *Numismatic Chronicle,* 1971, pp. 253-260.

Metcalf, D.M. "Silver and tin in the Byzantine trachy coinages", *Revue belge de numismatique,* 123, 1977, pp. 107-131.

___. "Byzantine scyphate bronze coinage in Greece", *Annual of the British School of Archaeology at Athens,* vol. 56, pp. 42-63.

Weller, H.L. "Eighteen Byzantine Scyphate Coins of the Late 1200s", *Numismatic Chronicle,* 1969, pp. 235-246.

Countermarks

Heraclius monogram c/m

Sicily SCL c/m

Heraclius eagle c/m

Countermarks are not seen all that frequently on these coins, and very rarely on coins other than bronze. Those most commonly encountered are the Heraclian monogram countermarks from Syracuse and the Levant, eagle countermarks during the time of Heraclius on earlier 6th century folles, Sicily countermarks on coins of the seventh century and countermarks of Constantine IV at the mint in Cyprus. Folles of Maurice Tiberius from Cherson were also countermarked during the Heraclian dynasty—apparently at Bosporos instead of Cherson.

Turkoman countermarks appear on 10th and 11th century folles—a great many were published in *The Mardin Hoard*— and Arab or Turkish countermarks also appear on some silver coins of the 11th century. Of course these latter examples are countermarked by another political entity.

Bibliography — Countermarks

Bendall, Simon. "An 'eagle' countermark of sixth century Byzantine coins", *Numismatic Chronicle*, 1976, p. 230.

Goehring, James E. "Two New Examples of the Byzantine 'Eagle' Countermark", *Numismatic Chronicle*, 1983, pp. 218-220.

Hebert, R.J. "Concerning Tenth to Twelfth Century Byzantine Folles with Islamic and other Countermarks", *Numismatic Circular*, 82:3, 1974, pp. 94-96 and 82:4, pp. 140-141 and 82:5, pp. 189-190.

Lowick, N.M., S. Bendall and P.D. Whitting. *The Mardin Hoard. Islamic Countermarks on Byzantine Folles*, London, 1977.

Weller, H. "Turkic Countermarks [on Byzantine coins]", *Numismatic Circular*, 83:12, 1975, pp. 475-477.

The Anonymous Folles

The "anonymous" folles are so-called because they do not bear the name or mark of any particular ruler. These coins were issued during the period between 969 and 1092 and include purely religious images and inscriptions. The first anonymous folles were issued by John I Tzimisces and they were struck in many varieties until the reform of Alexius.

The early attempts to classify these coins by type go back to Wroth's BMC catalogue in 1908, and probably earlier. The bibliography at the end of this section list the major articles since then that are pertinent. Margaret Thompson, using coins from the excavations in Athens, was the first to arrange these types chronologically by evidence of overstriking. Since then, several new types have been added and at least one of these has subsequently been removed (Class N). What has evolved is an alphabetical arrangement of the coins by type, with tentative attributions to ruler.

Class A is normally divided into three subclasses A1, A2 and A3. These are characterized by differences in size and details of the subsidiary elements. For a thorough discussion of the subclasses of this type, and their chronology,

Class A

Class B

Class C

Class D

Class E

Class F

Class G

Class H

Class I

Class J

see William E. Metcalf's article listed in the bibliography to this section.

Being the first of the anonymous types, it seems fitting somehow that the obverse of Class A bears a portrait of the popular Christ Pantocrator. The varieties of this type were probably issued through the reign of Romanus III.

Class B is similar, but with the addition of a cross on the reverse. Grierson lists this issue as being struck under Michael IV.

Class C is attributed to the same emperor. It bears on the obverse an icon of Christ standing. It seems this icon was particularly venerated by Michael's wife Zoe (see Zoe under "Gallery of Emperors and Empresses").

Class D features Christ enthroned, reflecting the concept of Rex Regnantium—"King of those who rule". Grierson assigns this class to Constantine IX.

Classes E and F were assigned to Constantine X. Class E revives the Pantocrator obverse, with a reverse similar to that of class A. Class F is like Class D except that the throne on Class D has a high back, and that on Class F has no back.

Glass G is assigned to Romanus IV. It features on the obverse a bust of Christ holding a scroll, and on the reverse a bust of the Virgin orans.

Class H is assigned to Michael VII. It portrays the

Pantocrator and a cross with two arms.

Class I has been attributed to Nicephorus III and is like the previous class but only one arm on the cross.

Classes J and K were struck during the reign of Alexius I Comnenus. The former portrays the Pantocrator with a cross behind his head but no halo. On its reverse is a cross with crescent below. The latter portrays the standard Pantocrator and a 3/4 length effigy of the Virgin orans.

Coins formerly published as Classes L and M are not actually coins from the empire at Constantinople, but from the independent empire at Trebizond. These are from a series including at least 12 such anonymous coins—see Bendall in the bibliography below.

The coins formerly published as Class N are not actually anonymous, and have been reattributed to Nicephorus Basilacius (see Gallery of Emperors and Empresses).

Class K

Class L

Class M

Bibliography — Anonymous Folles

Bellinger, Alfred. *Anonymous Byzantine Bronze Coinage*, ANS NNM 35, NY, 1928.

Bendall, Simon. "More Byzantine Anonymous Bronze Folles", *The Celator*, 12:11, November, 1998, p. 6ff.

Metcalf, D.M. "Interpretation of the Byzantine 'Rex Regnantium' Folles of Class 'A' c. 970-1030", *Numismatic Chronicle*, 1970, pp. 199-219.

Metcalf, William E. "Early Anonymous Folles from Antioch and the Chronology of Class A", *ANSMN* 21, 1976, pp. 109-128.

Thompson, Margaret. *The Athenian Agora*, Vol. II, *Coins: Roman-Venetian*, Princeton, 1954, pp. 109-115.

Whitting, P.D. "The anonymous Byzantine bronze", *Numismatic Chronicle*, 1955, pp. 89-99.

Wroth, W. *Catalogue of the Byzantine Coins in the British Museum*, II, London, 1908, pp. 480ff.

Iconography

Although the "Byzantine" empire is treated politically and historically as an entity separate from the empire of the Romans, the dividing line is not at all clear. The city of Rome had already lost its position of preeminence in the fourth century. Therefore, the differences that one might point to had already evolved by the fateful year 476—which traditionally marks the "Fall of Rome". In spite of the fact that Rome no longer served as the central administrative center of the empire, there really were not any radical changes. In coinage, the main difference between what we consider Roman and that which followed it, is largely a matter of fabric and style. But, that too was evolutionary.

In sixth and seventh century coinage there are many reminders of the past. Most notable of these is the predilection toward representation of the imperial bust. In a few instances, there is even an attempt to revive the venerable Roman portrait. Amidst radical stylization, prompted by a spiritualistic milieu, we find wonderfully sculptural profiles of Anastasius, Justinian and even Maurice Tiberius. These are particularly evident in the fractional gold issues, but are not unknown among the bronzes. Imperial dress and accouterments are largely unchanged from Roman models during this period, and numismatic inscriptions tend to reflect traditional Roman institutions.

Over time, the bronze coinage exhibits less concern for aesthetic qualities and during the reigns of Heraclius and Constans II it becomes undeniably crude. A surge of religious fervor led to the portrayal of Christ on gold coins of Justinian II (AD 685-695 and 705-711). It is ironic that this incipient change in iconography coincided with the advent of Iconoclasm—which prevailed from the end of the seventh century to the middle of the ninth. Although imperial figures continue to be seen on coinage of this period, no further images of Christ were to appear until AD 842. Christ's portrait was reintroduced, oddly enough, on coins of the emperor we know as Michael the Drunkard. Being only an infant at the time, the decision was obviously that of his regent mother Theodora.

Fortunately, by this time the fabric and striking of bronze coins had improved—as had the care with which they were designed. Consequently, there were some very attractive types issued in the late 9th and 10th centuries. Imperial representations were gradually subordinated in favor of religious icons and often the emperor was depicted as a minor figure in the iconographic scheme.

Toward the later years of the empire, the coinage bears an almost exclusively religious content and takes on the appearance of an emergency coinage as the empire disintegrated politically and financially.

Vestiges of Imperial Portraiture

Portraiture, at least in official art, had all but vanished by the sixth century. By then it was no longer fashionable to show the realistic effigy of a ruler. Still, we find lingering traces of the old Roman portrait style in the occasional artist's rendering.

Anastasius I, AD 491-518
AE 20 nummia
Constantinople mint

Phocas, AD 602-610
AE 5 nummia
Catania mint

Justinian I, AD 527-565
AE 20 nummia
Rome mint

Leontius, AD 695-698
AE 40 nummia
Constantinople mint

The Antithesis of Portraiture

The essence of spiritualism is that all things physical hinder the cosmic connection. Therefore, the depiction of realistic effigies was seen as an impious display of vanity.

Justinian I, AD 527-565
AE 40 nummia
Constantinople mint

Tiberius II Constantine
AD 578-582, AE 40 nummia
Nicomedia mint

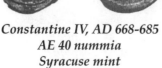

Constantine IV, AD 668-685
AE 40 nummia
Syracuse mint

Theophilus, AD 829-842
AE 40 nummia
Syracuse mint

Spiritualism, as a philosophy, may be traced back to the teachings of Plotinus about AD 250. From this came the belief that beauty itself is ultimate simplicity. That is, real beauty is in the soul and the body merely disrupts the perception of that beauty. Therefore, abstraction is beauty and a channel to the soul. For a stimulating analysis of this concept see Warren G. Moon and Paul Plass, "Influence of Plotinus led to 'hard style' in coinage", in *The Celator*, 3:11, November, 1989.

Numismatic art found its most abstract expression in the coinage of the Late Palaeologan period. Christopher T. Connell has pointed this out most graphically in his article "Icon of Christ on coins of John VIII is remarkable for its abstract imagery", *The Celator*, 5:12, December, 1991. Having analyzed the composition of the stavrata obverse, he finds that it is composed of "three circles, two semicircles, and thirty lines." Clearly, this is the ultimate in beauty—by some peoples' standards.

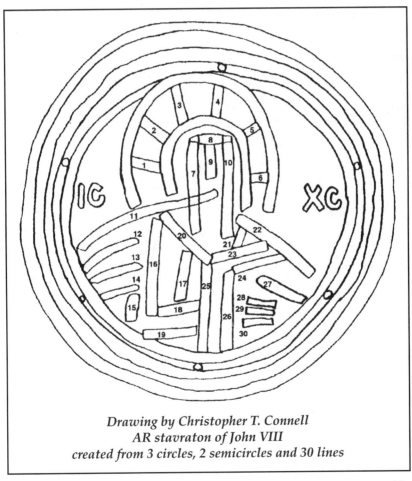

Drawing by Christopher T. Connell
AR stavraton of John VIII
created from 3 circles, 2 semicircles and 30 lines

Imperial Dress

The subject of imperial dress is complex, and it is not possible to fully explain here the many nuances nor the lengthy evolution of various garments as bearers of meaning. The topic is treated at great length in "The Symbolism of the Imperial Costume as Displayed on Byzantine Coins" by George P. Galavaris (*ANSMN* VIII, 1958, pp. 99-117). Let us merely say that all of the imperial garments were specific and well understood expressions of the ruler's legal and divine authority and purpose. The importance of imperial dress was such that an *Eidikos*, master of the imperial wardrobe, was an integral part of the court.

When we describe an imperial figure as "a crowned bust wearing chlamys" we are not talking about a common mode of dress, like a man in a gray flannel suit. The imperial *chlamys,* with a tunic under it, was the imperial state costume originally worn by the Roman consul. It was given to the emperor at his coronation and was worn as a symbol of rank and authority—the right to rule. The *trabea* was also a Roman consular or triumphal garb, which eventually became the Greek *loros.* By the post–iconoclastic period, the loros had fully evolved as the manifestation of Christ on earth. It symbolized the burial and resurrection of Christ, and the wearing of it by the emperor alluded to a partnership with God to rule the mortal kingdom. The *paludamentum* was a military cloak used for public appearances. It signified the emperor as *dominus mundi,* lord of the world, with the anointment of Christ. Finally, the *sakkos,* a long black undergarment signified the mystery of the imperial person.

When the emperor performed various of-

Consuls wearing chlamys from a 5th - 6th century diptych (Dalton)

ficial functions related to church or state he changed his dress appropriately, so as to convey the proper image. The dress of the imperial figure was so important that treatises were written on the proper wear of these various garments (Psellus notes that when Michael Kalaphates took sanctuary in the Studite monastery he changed into the clothes of a suppliant).

In the first illustration shown here, Tiberius II Constantine wears the traditional Roman trabea of a consul. In his right hand he holds the mappa, a napkin which was used by the consul to signal the start of the public games. In his left he holds an eagle-tipped scepter. His crown includes the imperial pendilia. That is, the decorated strands hanging to each side.

Over time, the jewelled trabea became larger, and its name was changed from the less popular Latin term to the Greek—loros. On the follis of Michael II and Theophilus, we see the latter (right) wearing a loros while his father wears the imperial chlamys. These two garments represent the political and religious aspects of the imperial persona. Subconsciously this suggests a unity of the emperor with God and also a unity between the two emperors, which paved the way for an unopposed succession, should the senior expire.

Finally, in the histamenon of Constantine IX, we see an example of the imperial sakkos worn beneath the loros. It is especially evident as drapery over the upper arms. Constantine holds a globus cruciger in his left hand and a scepter in his right, both symbols of the authority to rule.

Tiberius II Constantine
wearing consular trabea
AD 578-582
AE 40 nummi, Constantinople

Michael II and Theophilus
AD 821-829
AE follis, Constantinople
Michael (left) wearing chlamys
and Theophilus wearing loros

Constantine IX, AD 1042-1055
AV histamenon, Constantinople
wearing loros and sakkos

1st reign

2nd reign

Representations of Christ on solidi of Justinian II

During the reign of Justinian II (AD 685-695 and 705-711), religious art found its way into coinage in a major way. For the first time, an icon of Christ was depicted on official coinage as a primary element of design. An icon is, by definition, a pictorial representation of Christ, the Virgin Mary, the archangels Michael or Gabriel, or the saints. Iconodules worshipped these entities through iconographic representations of them. Iconoclasts opposed the worship or veneration of icons. The episode referred to historically as *Iconoclasm* did not arise within the church at Constantinople entirely as a matter of philosophy, but also as a matter of political necessity. By the late seventh century, when the movement to ban images of Christ began, the church was torn by internecine conflict.

The most pressing issue was opposition to the growing cult of icon veneration. The Patriarch at Constantinople was, after all, an *ecumenical* Patriarch. That is, he was Patriarch of the church throughout the entire world—and many of the outlying sects adamantly opposed the veneration of icons. Emperor Leo III's opposition to the cult initiated the crises when in the year 726 he ordered removal of certain icons. His motivation was apparently an act of appeasement to the Monophysites, who extolled the divine rather than human nature of Christ; to the Manicheans, who considered all material possessions (including religious art) evil; and to the ever growing population of Muslims, whose teachings rejected any representation of the human form. All of these factions were strong forces in the East.

What he did not fully appreciate was the tremendous affection with which the people of Constantinople, and European provinces, held their

Theophilus, AD 829-842, AR miliarense inscribed Basileus Romaion

religious icons. The destruction of venerable paintings, statues and mosaics created great dissention and serious riots. One agent sent by Leo to remove a statue of Christ over the gate to the Imperial Palace was slain on the spot. Later, the entire province of Hellas revolted and sent an army against Constantinople.

In spite of the unpopularity of the proclamations against icons, a succession of emperors supported this policy, with varying fervor, for more than a century. During this period, from the accession of Leo III to the death of Theophilus, numismatic art also reflects the general prohibition. It is during this time that we find on coins abundant representations of the cross, but no images of Christ or the saints. It should be said that the empress Irene moderated the persecution of iconodules (venerators of icons) but the policies basically remained in force nonetheless. Leo V (AD 813-820) renewed the persecutions, and as a result was assassinated during Christmas day high mass at the church of The Holy Wisdom, (Hagia Sophia). The emperor Theophilus was also an iconoclast, highly trained in religious doctrine, but refrained from persecutions and thereby avoided a similar fate.

Finally, the iconodules won the day with rhetoric and logical debate. They managed to effect the formulation of a doctrine that clearly defined the nature of Christ and the nature of icons. The icons were finally restored under the empress Theodora (regent for her son Michael III) in March of AD 843. Coins struck after that date are replete with depictions of Christ, the Virgin Mary, saints and angels. The restoration of icons is referred to as the "Triumph of Orthodoxy" and is still celebrated as a religious holiday, on the first Sunday of Lent, by the Greek Orthodox Church.

The defeat of Iconoclasm was more than simply a religious doctrinal issue laid to rest. It was a confirmation of the principle that the church could not be dominated by the imperial court. The recognition of Patriarchal power held major significance for development of the orthodox religion. This growth of political power led to the eventual schism of the Eastern and Western churches. Within the empire, the end of iconoclasm marked a new era of cooperation and a renewal of attention to foreign affairs which had suffered during the internal strife.

Bust of Christ (x1.5)
AV solidus, AD 856-866
Michael III, "the drunkard"

The Pantocrator

The earliest depiction of Christ on a coin seems to be on a solidus of AD 450-457 where He is included in the marriage scene of Marcian and Pulcheria (MacDonald, *Coin Types, their origin and development*, pp. 233-235). However, the first real *portrait* of Christ appears on coinage during the reign of Justinian II (see illustration on page 26). By that time, the image of Christ holding a gospel book was already a standard icon in church liturgy. It appears at least as early as the sixth century, in the illuminated manuscript of Cosmas Indicopleustes, and probably in a variety of other art forms. Later, it became a very popular subject for church dome mosaics, as the emotional impact of a stern Savior was all the more enhanced by this lofty perspective. Among the many famous examples which survive are those at the churches of St. Luke in Phocis; Chora in Istanbul and Daphne (near Athens).

The concept of Pantocrator as judge or "Jehovah", comes from the oriental view of Christ as opposed to the more western view of Christ as "Redeemer". The idea of a ruler of the universe was deeply ingrained in the culture of the Greek people, reaching back to the *pambasileus* Zeus—who bestowed the right to rule on Hellenistic kings. It should not be too surprising that Greek and Eastern Christians embraced this nature of Christ. Nor should it surprise us that after Iconoclasm had run its course, the image of the Pantocrator returned to become a major iconographic element throughout most of the later empire. The Pantocrator was even depicted above the imperial throne, implying that judgement on earth is derived from divine wisdom.

The Pantocrator : Church of Chora - Istanbul

Rex Regnantium

The semantic difference between Pantocrator (the original idea of Christ as "King of Kings") and Rex Regnantium ("King of those who rule") may seem slight, but it embodies an important nuance. As Pantocrator, Christ rules the entire universe, as well as all of mankind—including kings. As Rex Regnantium, Christ rules his earthly subjects through the emperor—his chosen instrument. The fact that these two terms, the first Greek and the second Latin, are virtually indistinguishable to the man on the street would suggest that they were more political than religious in nature. The iconography associated with these carefully articulated roles of Christ also differed. The former has already been discussed, the latter consisted of the portrayal of Christ enthroned.

In order for the concept of the emperor as the divine instrument of Christ to gain legitimacy, it was important that Christ himself should be represented on the imperial throne. Having established this mental image, it was easy enough to represent the emperor as the mortal manifestation of that power. This imagery of Christ enthroned was introduced on the coinage of Basil I along with the inscription +IhS XPS REX REϛNANTIЧM+. It was characterized by a distinctive throne with a lyre-shaped back. This throne, which was shared by Christ and the emperors Basil I through Constantine VII, helped make it clear that the person of the emperor was divinely empowered and was to be venerated as such. Under Constantine VIII, the Rex Regnantium title appears with the Pantocrator iconography, suggesting that the philosophical transition was complete.

Leo VI, AE follis

Mosaic: Emperor / Christ (Hagia Sophia Narthex)

bASILEVS RWMAIWN

The imperial title *Basileus* (broadly meaning "ruler") is a Greek term stemming from the days of the Athenian archons—if not earlier. It was a common title of Hellenistic kings, and from its inception bore religious overtones. The term became popular in Constantinople as an imperial title which held significance to the Greek speaking population, in contrast to the literal, and stilted, translation of Latin titles. This became especially so during the reign of Leo III, the "Isaurian" (AD 717-741) who was a Greek speaking ruler and brought a predominantly Greek view to the throne. From that time on, the title Basileus is seen with increasing frequency on coinage.

The implications of this Greek language layered on Roman tradition have led to the modern question "What is a Byzantine?" One view, which we find rational, was articulated by Clifton Fox in an article written for *The Celator* (March, 1996). That article was quoted in abridged form in Volume I of this series. One section of the article which was not quoted there, deals with the title *Basileus*. We provide here the words of Professor Fox which so well explain the nuances of that title.

[The word *Basileus* deserves a history of its own. In classical Greece, Basileus meant "King," equivalent to the Latin "Rex." From the time of Emperor Augustus [died 14 AD], Greeks called the Roman Emperor by the name Basileus. In the Latin language, of course, the Emperor was never called Rex, which was offensive to Roman Republican sensibilities: the Emperors were, in theory, chiefs of a Republican government. Roman Republicanism notwithstanding, the use of Basileus became standard among Greek speaking Romaioi to describe the Emperor. No way existed to translate the titles of *Imperator* or *Augustus* into Greek that did not sound contrived or ridiculous. The word *Autocrator* was coined to translate "Imperator."; *Sebastos* stood as the parallel to "Augustus," but neither Autocrator nor Sebastos acquired popular currency. Instead, the pretense developed that Basileus meant Emperor instead of King. Romaioi commenced to use the Latin "Rex" to mean "King" in reference to non-Roman rulers of lesser rank than their own Emperor. The new usage of Basileus gained formal status much later. In the seventh century, Emperor Heraclius first employed Basileus in Greek language legal documents as his official title, but the word only replaced "Augustus" on the coinage in the Isaurian era [717-802].

One impetus to the adoption of the new title came from the Empress Irene [797-802]. She had been the wife of Emperor Leo IV [775-780]. After Leo's death, Irene assumed power as the regent of their infant son Constantine VI . In 797, Irene deposed and blinded her son to prevent his achievement of power at adulthood. Irene declared herself ruler in her own right, a claim that no woman had ever made before in Imperial history. In advancing her novel claim, Irene faced a difficulty of nomenclature. The Imperial title Augustus was, of course, male. Irene could not call herself Augustus without appearing ridiculous. The female form of Augustus, *Augusta* might have served the required purpose, except that Augusta had signified in the past the wife of the Emperor or other important female relation, not a legitimate ruler. The usage of Augusta to designate female members of the Imperial family dated back to the early years of the Empire. Emperor Augustus' widow Livia accepted the name "Julia Augusta" from the Senate in 14 AD. Throughout a span of close to eight hundred years, Augusta had not ever been suggestive of a ruler in her own right; the existence of an Augusta implied the existence of an Augustus. Irene had no desire to remind the Romaioi of her son Constantine. Therefore, Irene's inscriptions uniformly eschewed the word Augusta. Instead, Irene elected to call herself by the female form of Basileus, that had in the past been employed by reigning Queens as well as consorts and mothers of Kings. The unabbreviated form of the inscription was: ERINH BASILISSH. Note the mixture of Latin and Greek letters. On coins, the abbreviated version ERINH BAS appeared in most cases. The stunning event of Irene's reign was the coronation at Old Rome of Frankish King Charlemagne [Carolus Rex Francorum] as Emperor in 800. Many authorities in the Latin speaking world had continued to recognize the Emperors at Constantinople as the legitimate Roman Emperors until Irene deposed her son in 797. In the eyes of the Latin West, the throne became vacant upon the removal of Constantine VI. Irene appeared objectionable on three counts: she was a woman, she had committed the heinous act of blinding her own son, and she adhered to Eastern religious practices, which the West rejected. Although Charlemagne, a Germanic tribesman [better to think of him as Karl instead of with the Frenchified Charlemagne], was no Roman, he had brought unity to much of Europe. Why should not he, instead of some Greek woman [Graeca], be Emperor? The Pope thought on these lines, and placed the Imperial crown on Charlemagne's head at Christmas, 800. After his coronation, Charlemagne called himself "Carolus Augustus Imperator Romanorum Gubernans Imperium" [Charles Augustus, Emperor governing the Domains of the Romans]. The authorities at Constantinople did not wish to recognize the claims of the Frankish upstart in the West, although political reality forced a compromise on the part of Emperor Michael I [811-813]. Michael's envoy from Constantinople saluted Charlemagne at his court in Aachen as "Basileus," that the Westerners translated with satisfaction as Emperor. Of course, the Greek speakers had room to live in the ambiguity of the word "Basileus." Back in Constantinople, Michael began to call himself [in unabbreviated form]: MIXAHL BASILEYS ROMAION [Michael, Roman Emperor]. Note the Greek "upsilon"[Y], "chi" [X] and "eta" [H]. On coins, the usual form was MIXAHL BAS ROM. Before this change, no Roman Emperor had ever used the word "Roman" in his official titles: the Emperor was simply the "Imperator Caesar Augustus." Diplomatists at Constantinople would soon argue that "Basileus Romaion" and "Basileus" were two different things.

In that view, "Basileus Romaion" stood as a superior and unique title reserved for the ruler at Constantinople. According to this clever theory, Michael had really conceded Charlemagne nothing except a royal title, "Basileus" in the sense of "King", equivalent to the Latin "Rex."]

———————————————

GALLERY OF
EMPERORS AND EMPRESSES
AD 491 — AD 1453

With the exception of the anonymous bronze folles of the mid 10th to mid 11th centuries, and a few isolated issues, Romaion coinage generally honors the reigning imperial ruler. It is, in this respect, much like its Roman predecessors. Earlier Greek coins, with the exception of those struck for Hellenistic Kings, tended to portray deities, heroes, personifications, and various objects of nature. Greek rulers were typically acknowledged in a rather obscure reverse legend or monogram. It is fitting, therefore, that we present the coinage of the Romaion people as a chronology of imperial types—a gallery if you will of political leaders. We hesitate to use the term "portrait gallery", as we did with the Romans in Volume III, because it would be a real stretch of the definition to call some of these representations portraits. Still, this is the method in which most collections of these coins are built. It is true that some collectors specialize in particular periods or mints, or in coins bearing on broader social or economic issues. But, like collectors of Roman coins the beginner in this series is likely to collect by ruler.

There are many rarities among the coins portrayed here, and one should keep in mind that the purpose of this gallery is not to create a "penny board" where one can attempt to match one-for-one the coins on display. It is merely to introduce the history and personalities of this culture as a very brief overview. It certainly is not an attribution guide, although it may well serve as an aid in this respect. We have included only those illustrations pertinent to the text. In the case of individual rulers, for example, we typically have reproduced the obverse or reverse as necessary to represent the individual. Where co-rulers have issued a coin, we have illustrated those rulers either independently or together, as they are typically seen on the coinage. In some cases, where iconographic details are significant, we have illustrated these as well. The photographs are presented at actual size unless indicated otherwise in the description.

It should be noted here that the inscriptions listed below each ruler's name in the heading are merely representative of what may actually be seen on the coinage. There are many variants of these legends which include references to associate rulers, titles and epithets. There are also many inconsistencies in the spelling and the formation of letters within coins of the same ruler and over time. The letter *Beta*, for example, in the word *Basileus* is often rendered with an open bottom, so that it ap-

33

pears to be an "R". Likewise, the Latin "d" abbreviating the word *Dominus* is rendered as ᴆ. Mixtures of upper and lower case letters are very common. The ruler's name appears sometimes on the obverse, sometimes on the reverse of the coin. Many of the emperors or empresses were given epithets or "nicknames" which reflected their family name, place of birth, notable deeds or physical features. For example, we find Pogonatus, "the bearded", Rhinotmetes, "slit-nosed", and Bulgaroctonos, "the Bulgar slayer". These epithets are mentioned in the headings after the ruler's name. An index to the personalities recorded appears at the end of the section (p. 122).

We have included a side-bar for each ruler listing the major mints at which coins were struck. Of course the serious collector will carefully evaluate the definitive references in this series, but this simple listing gives the reader a sense of the political and financial activity that accompanied a given reign. We also have included, as in Volume III of this series, a short bibliography for each ruler. We have found this format to be very useful in locating references for a particular ruler or historical period. It is inevitable that certain sources provide more biographical information and others more technical numismatic information. We have purposely included some of each. Biographical information on rulers is often available only in general works. In this regard, we have limited our references to a few readily available sources to make it easier for readers to locate these references. Hence, the frequent references to Goodacre, Jenkins, Wroth, and others which we have found interesting or informative. There are, of course, many other possible sources and these are not necessarily the "best" for any given ruler. Goodacre, for example, is very colorful and not always to be trusted for factual detail— but it is delightful to read. Grierson is exceptionally precise and technical, but it is impossible to read in a biographical sense. What we have tried to do here is present a mix of the available material. It will be noticed that we have included the complete bibliographic information in each gallery vignette. While this is admittedly redundant, we have felt that each vignette should more or less stand alone—so that the reader is not made to search for earlier bibliographic citations to obtain needed information. We also have avoided abbreviations when possible, but the American Numismatic Society Museum Notes and Numismatic Studies (ANSMN and ANSNS) are abbreviated throughout.

Today, the Internet is a wonderful new source of historical and numismatic information. In Volume I, we listed many internet sources only to find that these sites often change addresses or content. Therefore, we will refrain from making specific suggestions here—but we highly recommend a web-search by appropriate keywords.

Additional bibliographies at the end of this volume list works of a more general nature or works related to specific numismatic problems which were not addressed earlier in the text.

Anastasius I
DN ANASTASIVS PP AVG

Anastasius was a *silentary* or high ranking administrator in the court of Zeno. Although he was not born "of noble blood", he was highly respected by the clergy—who by this time were very influential. On the death of Zeno, since the emperor left no heir, there was disagreement over who should be elevated to the throne. As a result, Zeno's wife Ariadne was allowed to select the successor.

Anastasius I, AD 491-518
AV solidus (x1.5)
Constantinople mint

She wisely chose a man of maturity and reason. Shortly after the coronation, Anastasius and Ariadne were married, thereby cementing his authority. Anastasius proved to be an administrator of superior ability, particularly in financial affairs. He greatly improved the size and stability of the imperial treasury, and in AD 498 instituted a major monetary reform. In addition to restoring the large bronze coin as a standard issue, Anastasius also established the relational system of bronze denominations which bore marks of value (M, K, I etc.) on the reverse. This system was employed until nearly the tenth century. He was an adherent of the sect of Christianity known as Monophysitism, which believed that in the person of Christ there was but a single divine nature. This deviation from the Orthodox view caused considerable unrest among the court and was a major source of distraction to his otherwise successful reign.

MINTS	
Constantinople	Nicomedia
Thessalonica	Antioch

BIBLIOGRAPHY

Fagerlie, J. M. "The first gold issue of Anastasius", *ANSMN* 13, 1967, p. 119-21.

Grierson, P. "The monetary reforms of Anastasius and their economic consequences", *Proceedings, International Numismatic Congress, Jerusalem, 1963*, pp283-302, Tel-Aviv and Jerusalem, 1967.

Kollgaard, Ron. "The Fall of Rome and the Early Byzantine Empire: Part 4, Anastasius I", *The Celator*, 07:03, March 1993, pp. 14 ff.

Metcalf, D.M. *The Origins of the Anastasian Currency Reform*, Chicago, 1969.

___. "Organization of the Constantinople mint for the follis of the Anastasian reforms", *Numismatic Chronicle*, 1961, pp. 131-143.

Shaw, A.B. "Byzantine Folles of Anastasius I", *The Numismatist*, 76, 1963, pp. 159-169.

Justin I
DN IVSTINVS PP AVG

Justin I, AD 518-527
AE 40 nummi

Justin I & Justinian I, AD 527
AV solidus (x1.5)

MINTS

Cherson	Cyzicus
Constantinople	Antioch
Thessalonica	Alexandria
Nicomedia	

Justin, born in AD 450, was an illiterate peasant from Thrace. He rose through the ranks of the army to the position of Commander of the Imperial Guard *(Excubitors)* in Constantinople. Although neither a learned man, nor a politician, he was able to manipulate the contenders hoping to succeed Anastasius—who left no successor. As a result, Justin himself was able to ascend the throne. He retained many of his unsophisticated ways, bringing to the palace with him a barbarian wife that was formerly his purchased slave.

Justin wisely sought the counsel of his nephew Justinian, who played an important part in administration of the empire. In April of 527, only months before the death of his uncle, Justinian was elevated to the rank of co-emperor, ensuring a peaceful succession.

Most references gloss over the reign of Justin and treat it as merely a prelude to that of Justinian. One of the more lively biographical sketches may be found in Goodacre.

BIBLIOGRAPHY

Bellinger, A. "The Gold of Justin I and Justinian I", *ANSMN* 12, 1966, pp. 90-2.
Grierson, P. "Anomalous pentanummia of Justin I", *The Numismatic Circular,* 75:9, 1967, p. 234.
Metcalf, William E. "The Joint Reign Gold of Justin I and Justinian I", *Studies in Early Byzantine Gold Coinage,* ANS Numismatic Studies 17, New York, 1988, pp. 19-27.
Vasiliev, A.A. *Justin the First, An Introduction to the Epoch of Justinian the Great,* Dumbarton Oaks Studies I, Cambridge, Massachusetts, 1950.

Justinian I
DN IVSTINIANVS PP AVG

Originally known as Peter, the nephew of Justin I was born in Illyria in AD 483. He was renamed Justinian and became a trusted advisor upon his uncle's accession, as well as heir to the throne. The reign of Justinian was long and successful. Most of the credit for his military success should be given however to his very competent generals. Belisarius stemmed the advance of Khusru II in the East and eliminated Gelimer and the Vandal presence in North Africa. Narses defeated the Goths in two major battles, and restored the Italian peninsula to the empire. Justinian was also fortunate to have the assistance of his wife Theodora, one of many strong and capable women who left their mark on the empire. She was an actress from the street and Justinian's choice of her as bride scandalized the aristocracy. As fate would have it, she was arguably the most brilliant queen and effective counsellor ever to wear the purple.

Justinian I, AD 527-565
AE 40 nummi

MINTS

Rome	Cyzicus
Ravenna	Antioch
Cherson	Theoupolis
Constantinople	Alexandria
Thessalonica	Carthage
Nicomedia	

Also, uncertain mints in: North Africa, Italy, Sicily and Spain

BIBLIOGRAPHY

Barker, J.W. *Justinian and the Later Roman Empire,* Univ. of Wisconsin, 1966.

Bellinger, A.R. "The Gold Coins of Justinian", *Archaeology,* III, 1950.

Browning, R. *Justinian and Theodora,* London, 1971.

Caramessini-Oeconomides, Mando. "An Unpublished Consular Solidus of Justinian I", *ANSMN* XII, 1966, pp. 75-78.

Fairhead, Niall. "Some pentanummia of Justinian I of Carthage", *Numismatic Circular,* 87:7-8, pp. 342-344, London, 1979.

Hahn, Wolfgang. "Italian small change of Justinian I", *Numismatic Circular,* 87:6, pp. 282-284, London, 1979.

Metcalf, D.M. "The metrology of Justinian's follis", *Num. Chron..,* 1960, pp. 209-219.

Ure, P.N. *Justinian and his Age,* Penguin Books, 1951.

DN IVSTINVS PP AVG

Justin II, AD 565-578
AV tremissis (x2)

Justin II and Tiberius
AV solidus (x1.5)

MINTS	
Rome	Theoupolis
Ravenna	Alexandria
Constantinople	Carthage
Thessalonica	
Nicomedia	Also, several
Cyzicus	uncertain mints

Like Justin I, Justinian chose his nephew as successor. Justin II was destined to serve as the consolidator of a shrinking empire, beset with problems on all fronts due to the ambitious expansion promoted by his uncle. If history has not unjustly maligned this emperor, he also was afflicted with serious emotional or psychiatric problems. At any rate, his wife Sophia became the real power behind the throne, and frequently shares the throne with him on coinage of the reign. She was a niece of the extraordinary Theodora, and apparently inherited the same strengths if not the dignity.

Justin's Commander of the Guard, Tiberius Constantine, was named Caesar in 574, and was crowned on September 26, 578 initiating their joint reign. It was to be short lived, as Justin died nine days later. The very rare issue illustrated here was struck for the coronation, depicting Justin II and Tiberius as co-emperors.

Sophia left the palace on Justin's death, but returned four years later on the accession of Maurice Tiberius. She did not take an active part in his reign, but apparently lived there in comfort for many years.

BIBLIOGRAPHY

Bellinger, A. "Silver with the name of Justin", *ANSMN* 12, 1966, pp. 96-8.
Ulrich-Bansa, O. "Note su alcune rare monete di rame dell'imperatore Giustino II (565-578)", *Numismatica*, 2, 1936, pp. 75-84.
Oman, C. "A Gold Solidus of A.D. 578: a Reattribution", *Numismatic Chronicle*, 1942, pp. 104-5.

Tiberius II Constantine
ꙩm TIb CONSTANT PP AVI

Tiberius II Constantine rose through the military and was elevated to the rank of Caesar in AD 574. He was crowned co-emperor in AD 578 just nine days before the death of Justin II and succeeded his benefactor without opposition.

I t was rumored that Sophia had designs of marrying the young Tiberius, but he was wed secretly to an unassuming matron from Daphnudium, and arranged to have her brought to Constantinople upon his accession. She was renamed Anastasia in a rite at the church of Hagia Sophia, but did not take an active role in state affairs like some of the other empresses of her time.

Tiberius II Constantine
AD 578-582, AE 40 nummi
Cyzicus mint

The reign of Tiberius was relatively uneventful, aside from some setbacks against the Avars. He was a popular ruler, noted for great liberality and fairness. He ruled four years, although in failing health. Before his death, Tiberius gave the hand of his daughter Constantina to Maurice, one of his most able generals. Maurice also took the name Tiberius.

MINTS	
Rome	Cyzicus
Ravenna	Theoupolis
Constantinople	Alexandria
Thessalonica	Carthage
Nicomedia	

Also, uncertain mints in: North Africa, Sicily and a "military mint".

Many of the coins of Tiberius II are characterized by the distinctive robe, scepter and mappa signifying the consulship—which he held alone.

BIBLIOGRAPHY

Hahn, W. "More About the Minor Byzantine Gold Mints from Tiberius II to Heraclius", *Numismatic Circular*, 87:12, 1979, pp. 552-555.
Whitting, P.D. "A New Transitional Byzantine Issue of A.D. 582", *Numismatic Chronicle*, 1960, pp. 133-135.
___. "An Unusual Pentanummia of Tiberius II", *Numismatic Circular* 57, 1949, p. 348.

dN MAVRIC TIbЄR PP AVC

Maurice Tiberius, AD 582-602
AE 40 nummi (x1.5)

MINTS

Rome	Thessalonica
Ravenna	Nicomedia
Catania	Cyzicus
Syracuse	Theoupolis
Cherson	Alexandria
Constantinople	Carthage

Also, uncertain mints in: North Africa, Sicily, Spain and a "military mint" at some unknown location

When Maurice came to the throne, he was already a popular figure due to his brilliant campaign against the Persians. An extensive coinage was issued under his reign, reflecting the success and prosperity of his administration. But his personal popularity suffered from the attention to state affairs and neglect of the familiar doles which his predecessors had handed over to the populace.

The army too became disgruntled and the emperor's lack of tact led to a mutinous rebellion under the ruffian Phocas. The citizens of Constantinople welcomed the approaching army of Phocas, and Maurice was forced to flee. Phocas was crowned emperor and immediately ordered the execution of Maurice, who had taken refuge in a church at Chalcedon. Ignoring this sanctuary, the entire family was gruesomely slain and their bodies were thrown into the sea.

BIBLIOGRAPHY

Bellinger, A.R. "The Helmet of Maurice", *ANSMN* 12, 1966, p. 106f.

Grierson, P. "Dated solidi of Maurice, Phocas and Heraclius", *Numismatic Chronicle*, 1950, pp. 49-70.

O'Hara, M.D. "An Interesting New Variety of the Crowned Bust Solidus of Maurice Tiberius for the Mint of Ravenna", *Numismatic Circular*, 38:10, 1980, p. 346.

Russell, James. "A Coin Hoard of Maurice Tiberius from Anemurium, Isauria", *ANSMN* 28, 1983, pp. 119-131.

Veglery, A. and G. Zacos. "More about the Bronze Coinage of Maurice", *Numismatic Circular*, 68, 1960, pp. 258-61.

DN TEODOSIVS PP A

The son of Maurice Tiberius and Constantia was born "in the purple", meaning that he was born while his father ruled as emperor. It was the first such birth in the Roman world in 200 years, and was the cause of much celebration in the city.

Theodosius ruled jointly with his father from AD 590 to 602 when they were overthrown and murdered during a military revolt. A series of gold and silver coins in his name were struck at the Carthage mint about the time of his coronation. The specimens illustrated here include an extremely rare solidus minted in the year 597/8 and an interesting family portrait coin, with Maurice and Constantia shown on the reverse and Theodosius on the obverse.

Another silver coin of this same period has on its obverse the bust of Theodosius, and on the reverse an inscription AMENITAS DEI which Goodacre translates as "the delight of God"—undoubtedly a reference to the young prince .

Certain bronze coins from Cherson with a standing figure in long robes and holding a tall cross, (4 pentanummia and 8 pentanummia) were for many years attributed to Maurice Tiberius (Sear 603-611). They have now been reattributed to Justin II and Sophia with Tiberius II.

Theodosius, AD 590-602
AV solidus (x2)
Carthage mint

AR 1/2 siliqua (x1.5)
Carthage mint
(Heraclius & Constantina
on reverse)

MINTS

Carthage

BIBLIOGRAPHY

Sear, David R. *Byzantine Coins and Their Values,* London, 1987, pp. 137-138 and p. 140.

Wroth, W. *Imperial Byzantine Coins in the British Museum,* reprint, Chicago, 1966, pp. xxii, 158-160.

ᴅN FOCAS PᴇRP AVG

Phocas, AD 602-610
AV solidus (x1.5), Constantinople

Phocas and Leontia
AE half-follis
dated AD 602/3, Cyzicus

MINTS

Uncertain Spain	Nicomedia
Catania	Cyzicus
Rome	Theoupolis
Ravenna	Jerusalem?
Constantinople	Alexandria
Thessalonica	Carthage

History has not been kind to Phocas. In fact, he has been viewed by most historians as the vilest creature ever to don the purple. His rebellion led to a period of serious disruption in the empire. Aristocrats were persecuted and the frontiers were left defenseless. The Persians swept through Asia Minor and actually reached Chalcedon on the shore of the Bosphorus. Ironically, this was the place where Phocas had Maurice Tiberius murdered only six years earlier.

According to a contemporary description, he was short and disfigured, with red hair and shaggy eyebrows. This seems to be borne out by the effigy on his coins—typically representing a coarse figure.

Phocas is depicted along with his wife Leontia on a bronze half-follis from Cyzicus. It is said that she was as bad as her husband.

When Heraclius finally appeared before Constantinople with his fleet, Phocas was given up by the people without opposition. It is said that he was beheaded and his body was dragged through the streets.

BIBLIOGRAPHY

Bendall, S. "A New Mint for Focas?", *Num. Circular*, 92:8 1984, pp. 256-7.

Grierson, P. "A Coin of the Emperor Phocas with the effigy of Maurice", *Numismatic Chronicle*, 1964, pp. 250.

___. "Solidi of Phocas and Heraclius", *Numismatic Chronicle*, 1959, pp. 131-154.

Leuthold, Enrico, Sr. & Jr. "Solidi leggeri do XXIII silique degli imperatori Maurizio Tiberio, Foca ed Eraclio", *Revista italiana di numismatica e scienze affini*, 62, 1960, pp. 146-154.

The Heraclian Dynasty

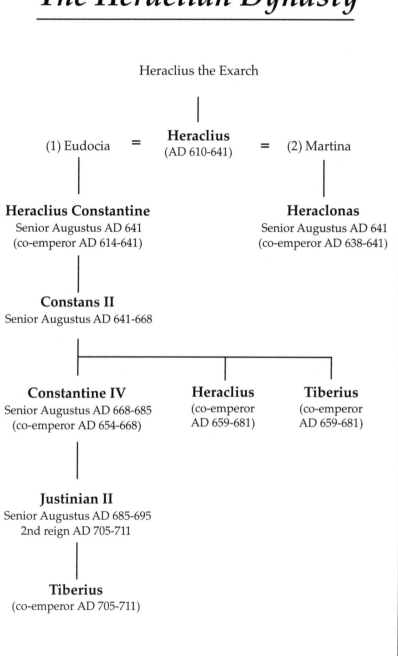

Heraclius the Exarch

|

(1) Eudocia   **=**   **Heraclius** (AD 610-641)   **=**   (2) Martina

Heraclius Constantine
Senior Augustus AD 641
(co-emperor AD 614-641)

Heraclonas
Senior Augustus AD 641
(co-emperor AD 638-641)

Constans II
Senior Augustus AD 641-668

Constantine IV
Senior Augustus AD 668-685
(co-emperor AD 654-668)

Heraclius
(co-emperor
AD 659-681)

Tiberius
(co-emperor
AD 659-681)

Justinian II
Senior Augustus AD 685-695
2nd reign AD 705-711

Tiberius
(co-emperor AD 705-711)

Revolt of the Heraclii
DN ЄRACΛIO CONSVΛI

Heraclius the exarch and son
AV solidus
AD 608-610, Alexandria?

MINTS

Sardinia?
Cyprus
Alexandretta
Alexandria
Carthage

The exarch at Carthage, Heraclius, and his son of the same name, led a popular rebellion against the repressive rule of Phocas in AD 608. The elder Heraclius was one of the leading generals under Maurice Tiberius, receiving the distinguished post in Carthage as a reward for his service. Over a period of two years, the two Heraclii marshalled their resources as the rebellion spread to the other outlying provinces. They assembled a sizeable fleet, which the younger then sailed against Constantinople. They stopped at islands and ports along the way gathering additional support and encouragement as well as extra forces. Upon his arrival, the people of the city opened the doors and welcomed Heraclius as a liberator. Phocas was deposed and executed, and his statue in the Hippodrome was publicly burned in damnation of his memory. The younger Heraclius was proclaimed emperor and crowned by the Patriarch.

The coin illustrated here exemplifies the unpretentious nature of their quest to unseat the tyrannical emperor. The Heraclii are depicted in consular garb, bareheaded and with inscriptions foregoing any claim to the throne. The fact that Heraclius the Younger did not associate his father with him as emperor would suggest that the Elder was indeed motivated by patriotism rather than ambition.

BIBLIOGRAPHY

Grierson, P. "The consular coinage of Heraclius and the revolt against Phocas of 608-610", *Numismatic Chronicle*, 1950, pp. 71-93.
Bendall, Simon. "A New Coin of the Revolt of Heraclius", *Numismatic Circular*, 94:7, 1986, p. 223.

Heraclius
dN hЄRACLI PЄRP AVG

Heraclius was 35 years old and unmarried when he deposed Phocas. Following his coronation, he immediately married a beautiful African girl named Fabia, who then, as queen, took the name Eudocia. She died two years later after giving the emperor a daughter and a son. Heraclius ruled solely from AD 610 to AD 613 and then jointly with his infant son Heraclius Constantine. His younger son, Heraclonas (by his second wife, and niece, Martina) was named co-emperor in AD 638.

Heraclius, AD 610-641
AV solidus (x1.5) Constantinople

Heraclius & Martina,
AR 1/2 siliqua (x2)

One of the most interesting episodes of his reign involved the loss and subsequent recovery of the True Cross. In 614, the Persians captured Jerusalem, burning the Church of the Holy Sepulchre and carrying off the Cross to Ctesiphon. In a series of Campaigns, Heraclius finally crushed the Persians and recovered the Cross, restoring it to Jerusalem.

Under the rule of Heraclius, Greek became the official language of state, supplanting the earlier Latin. It is at this point that we may truly refer to the Eastern Romans as "Romaion".

MINTS	
Catania	Seleucia Isauriae
Rome	Isaura
Ravenna	Jerusalem
Cherson	Alexandria
Constantinople	Carthage
Thessalonica	Uncertain mints in
Nicomedia	Spain, Sicily & Cyprus
Cyzicus	

BIBLIOGRAPHY

Connell, Christopher T. "Coins of Herakleios offer the greatest variety of any Byzantine emperor", *The Celator,* 06:10, Oct. 1992, pp. 6 ff.

Kollgaard, Ron. "Heraclius: the first basileus", *The Celator,* 10:01, Nov. 1996, pp. 6-20.

Matagne, Léon. "Le numéraire d'Heraclius", *Revue de belge de numismatique,* 188, 1972, pp. 93-108.

Sebêos. *Hist. d'Héraclius,* translated to French by F. Macler, Paris, 1904.

⊃N CONStANtINYS PP AV / dN hЄRACLI PЄRP AVG

*Heraclius with
Heraclius Constantine
and Heraclonas
AV solidus, Constantinople*

MINTS

Constantinople
Ravenna

(These mints are for the coins of Constantine and Heraclonas as senior Augustus. See the mints of Heraclius for issues of their joint reign.)

Heraclius Constantine, the infant son of Heraclius and Fabia Eudocia, was named co-ruler with his father in AD 613. After the death of Heraclius in 641, the consumptive youth (sometimes referred to as Constantine III) ruled jointly with his brother Heraclonas for a period of 100 days before succumbing to his illness.

Heraclonas survived his father and his half-brother to become senior Augustus on April 20, 641. He was only about 15 years old at the time and still under the strong influence of his mother Martina. After only five months in office, he was forced to elevate Constans II, the son of Heraclius Constantine, to the rank of co-emperor. In October of that same year, Heraclonas and his mother were deposed and banished to the island of Rhodes. In the oriental practice of the day, her tongue was slit and his nose was cut off. This was the first instance of the barbaric practice which would later become commonplace.

Heraclius Constantine and Heraclonas were depicted along with their father on many coins struck during their joint reign. It is not certain which, if any, of those variants might be attributed to their later reign. Several controversial attributions of this nature have been offered, but all are based on interpretive rather than epigraphical evidence.

BIBLIOGRAPHY

Grierson, P. *Byzantine Coins*, Berkeley, 1982, pp. 84-94.
Ostrogorsky, George. *History of the Byzantine State*, Rutgers, 1957, pp. 112-114.
Vasiliev, A.A. *History of the Byzantine Empire, 324-1453*, Univ. of Wisconsin, 1952, p. 193.
Whitting, P.D. *Byzantine Coins*, London, 1973, pp. 137-146.

ᴆⵌ CONStAͶtINⵣS PP AV

The son of Heraclius Constantine, called Constans II, was only eleven years old when his father's half-brother Heraclonas was deposed and exiled. The empire faced serious challenges during his reign. The Muslim expansion was uncontrollable and Egypt and Rhodes were lost. The Slavs also constituted a threat, and there were civil uprisings in Africa. Mostly through good fortune, Constans survived the difficulties and ruled for 27 years. He established a new system of provincial government called *themes*, which were districts under the control of a military governor.

His wife's name is unrecorded, but his sons Constantine IV, Heraclius and Tiberius all appear with their father on coins. In 662 Constans abruptly relocated his administration to Syracuse in Sicily—much to the dismay of the people and the Senate. He later sent for his family, but the Senate refused to let them leave fearing he would reestablish a new capital. His death was incredibly bizarre. At the age of 39, Constans was killed in his bath by a servant who struck him with a marble soap dish!

Constans II, AD 641-668
AE 40 nummi (x1.5), Syracuse

Heraclius and Tiberius
AE follis reverse (x1.5)

MINTS	
Syracuse	Constantinople
Naples	Cherson
Rome	Alexandria
Ravenna	Carthage
Thessalonica	

BIBLIOGRAPHY

Bates, G. E. "Constans II or Heraclonas? An Analysis of the Constantinopolitan Folles of Constans II", *ANSMN*, 17, 1971, pp. 141-61.

Bendall, Simon. "A New Sicilian Half Follis of Constans II", *Numismatic Circular*, 89:2, 1981, p. 38f.

Ostrogorsky, George. *History of the Byzantine State*, Rutgers, 1957, pp. 114-123.

ꞩn MEZEꞩIYꞩ AVY

Mezezius, AD 668-669
AV solidus (x2), Syracuse

MINTS
Syracuse

The murder of Constans was probably not an act of rage, or insanity, as is sometimes suggested—but rather part of a conspiracy hatched by the aristocracy in Constantinople. On his death, the army in Sicily proclaimed an Armenian noble by the name of Mezezius as emperor.

His coinage, limited to a gold series and struck only at the Syracuse mint, is very rare. The fact that there was some connection with the capital is borne out by the style of these issues which are very Constantinopolitan. It is conceivable that the dies were cut at Constantinople, and carried to Syracuse, even while Constans was still alive. These coins were initially assigned to the reign of Constantine IV, as Barbarous issues, until a specimen with full clear inscription was discovered in the 1970s. It was then that others were recognized as coins of this usurper. Since then, a semissis has also been published by Philip Grierson. It is likely that other types are yet to be found. Berk lists only six solidi known, but others have probably surfaced since then. Mezezius ruled only a few months before being captured and executed by the Exarch of Ravenna. According to some historians, the capture and execution of Mezezius came at the hands of Constantine IV, the son of Constans. However, this point has been argued (see the footnote in Ostrogorsky, below). Information about the usurper, his rise and his fall, is scanty to say the least.

BIBLIOGRAPHY

Grierson, P. "A semissis of Mezezius (668-9)", *Numismatic Chronicle*, 1986, pp. 231-232.
___. Byzantine Coins, Berkeley, 1982, p. 139.
Ostrogorsky, George. *History of the Byzantine State*, Rutgers, 1957, p. 123, + fn.
Sear, David R. *Byzantine Coins and Their Values*, London, 1987, p. 230.

ᴐᴨ CONStANtINYS PP AYɠ

Constantine IV was eighteen years old when his father was murdered in Sicily. He inherited the throne and associated his younger brothers Heraclius and Tiberius with him as co-emperors. It is said that he allowed his beard to grow after his father's death and thereby acquired the epithet Pogonatus ("the bearded").

One of the great events of Constantine's reign was the invention of "Greek Fire" or napalm. Working like a modern flamethrower, the weapon was mounted on ships and completely routed the Arab fleet which was blockading Cyzicus. This was followed up by a crushing land victory which drove the Arabs to a truce.

He also presided personally over the Sixth Ecumenical Council which ended the Monothelete controversy and reunited the Eastern church.

Constantine IV issued a fairly large series of coinage, mostly at mints in the west. Although the Arab threat had been reduced, the Eastern possessions which supported earlier mints had not been recovered.

Constantine IV
AD 668-685, AV solidus (x1.5)

Constans II & Constantine IV
AD 654-668, AV solidus (x1.5)

MINTS
Syracuse
Naples
Rome
Ravenna
Constantinople
Carthage

BIBLIOGRAPHY

Berk, Harlan J. "Constantine IV folles are reassessed: Two new classes identified" *The Celator*, 06:12, December 1992, pp. 24ff.

Weller, H.L. "A Coin of Constantine IV re-attributed from Constantinople to Carthage", *Numismatic Chronicle*, 1983, pp. 220-221.

IUStINIANUS PЄ AV

Justinian II, AV solidus (x1.5) AD
1st reign, AD 685-695,
Constantinople

Justinian II and Tiberius
2nd reign, AD 705-711
AV solidus, Constantinople

MINTS	
Sardinia	Ravenna
Syracuse	Constantinople
Naples	Carthage
Rome	

Justinian II was the son of Constantine IV, and inherited the empire at the impetuous age of 16. His uncles, Heraclius and Tiberius, had been deposed before the death of his father and Justinian ascended the throne as sole ruler.

His reign started well enough. The general Leontius subdued Spain and Ilyria; the Arabs signed a new treaty of peace favorable to Constantinople; and enormous losses were inflicted on the Bulgarians and Slavs. However, in 695, Justinian was deposed by Leontius, mutilated and exiled to Cherson. From this he gained the epithet *Rhinotmetes* meaning "slit-nosed". Regaining the throne in 705, Justinian launched a vendetta to take revenge on all who had opposed him in his first reign. He associated his son Tiberius with him as co-emperor, and the youth appears on coins of the second reign.

Numismatically, Justinian's claim to fame is the introduction of the portrait of Christ on his coinage. Most coins of this emperor are collected for that reason.

Justinian and his six-year-old son were executed following a rebellion of the army and installation of Philippicus Bardanes as emperor.

BIBLIOGRAPHY

Breckenridge, J.D. *The Numismatic Iconography of Justinian II*, ANS NNM 144, NY, 1959.

Fairhead, Niall. "A new silver coin of Justinian II of Carthage", Numismatic Chronicle, 1979, pp. 210-211.

Goodacre, Hugh. *A Handbook of the Coinage of the Byzantine Empire*, London, 1964 (reprint), pp. 114-115.

Leontius

D LEON PE AV

Leontius, a man of obviously greater military than political skills, came to power from his position as Strategus of the Hellas theme (Vasiliev lists him from Isauria). He came to power with the support of the party of the Blues. This was the upper class or aristocratic political party which Justinian had opposed (perhaps the origin of the term "blue-blood"). The party of the lower class was called the Greens. These parties were organized along religious as well as social lines.

Whether through his lack of ability or a lack of good fortune, Leontius ruled only three years before suffering the same fate as the man he displaced. During his reign there were constant uprisings within the empire and serious defeats abroad.

The Arabs took Carthage in 698, driving out the Roman army. As the troops made their way back to Constantinople, fearful of the emperor's reaction to their retreat, they proclaimed the admiral of the fleet, Apsimarus, emperor. On arriving at the city, the rebels overtook the palace and installed their new basileus on the throne. Leontius too had his nose slit and was sent to a monastery. This has to be a classic example of that old phrase "What goes around, comes around".

Leontius, AD 695-698
AV solidus (x1.5)

MINTS
Sardinia
Syracuse
Naples
Rome
Ravenna
Constantinople

BIBLIOGRAPHY

Ostrogorsky, George. *History of the Byzantine State,* Rutgers, 1957, pp. 140-141.

Sear, David R. *Byzantine Coins and Their Values,* London, 1987, p. 258-262.

Vasiliev, A.A. *History of the Byzantine Empire, 324-1453,* Univ. of Wisconsin, 1952, p. 193.

Walker, D.R. "A copper coinage for Leontius I", *The Numismatic Circular,* 75:10, 1967, pp. 264-265.

D tIbERIYS PE AV

Tiberius III, AD 698-705
AV solidus (x1.5)
Constantinople mint

MINTS

Sardinia
Syracuse
Naples
Rome
Ravenna
Constantinople

When he ascended the throne, with the help of the defeated army from Carthage and the city militia of the lower class (Greens) in Constantinople, Apsimar took the more recognizable and prestigious name Tiberius. He also took vengeance on the Arabs rather than the court at Constantinople. Appointing his able brother Heraclius as commander in the East, Tiberius enjoyed the fruits of victory in Cilicia, Antioch and Cyprus. This not only brought peace to these regions, it added huge revenues to the imperial treasury. In spite of his success, the people were never forgetful that Tiberius was a usurper.

Meanwhile, Justinian II had escaped from Cherson and joined a tribe of Turks known as Khazars. He married the sister of the Khan, and induced the neighboring Bulgar king to provide an army, then marched on Constantinople where his appearance raised such alarm that Tiberius fled from the palace and was captured.

Tiberius and the former emperor Leontius (who was still being held in a monastery) were brought to the Hippodrome where they were publicly humiliated, then dragged through the streets and beheaded. The general, Heraclius, and his leading officers were also brought to the city where they were hanged. The people had their legitimate emperor back—and a new reign of terror!

BIBLIOGRAPHY

Goodacre, Hugh. *A Handbook of the Coinage of the Byzantine Empire*, London, 1964 (reprint), pp. 120-121.
Limbourg, H.K. "A Half Tremissis of Tiberius III Absimarus, AD 698-705", *Numismatic Circular*, 86:1, 1978, p. 14.
Ostrogorsky, George. *History of the Byzantine State*, Rutgers, 1957, pp. 140-143.

☩N FIL€PICЧS MЧLTЧS AN

Bardanes was the family name of an Armenian general who used his unorthodox religious views as a basis for overthrowing the increasingly unpopular Justinian II in 711. His reign, was one of luxury and pleasure with little attention to the needs of the empire. At Rome, the authority of Philippicus was supposedly rejected due to his Monothelete association—but coins from the Rome mint are known nonetheless.

Philippicus, AD 711-713
AV solidus (x1.5)
Constantinople mint

His reign was very brief. As one story goes, a small group of dissidents managed to gain entrance to his personal quarters after he had retired in an intoxicated state from a birthday party in his honor. They blinded and deposed Philippicus before he was really aware of what was happening. According to other

MINTS
Syracuse
Rome
Ravenna
Constantinople

accounts, he was overthrown by a military revolt of the Opsikion theme—of course the two accounts may be related. Military coups did not always require the presence of an army at the city gates.

Apparently not involved in any conspiracy, the Senate appointed the secretary to Philippicus as his successor. The deposed emperor was taken to a monastery. The details of the reign of Philippicus are vague, and we have few sources to rely on. The coins themselves, although struck at several mints and in numerous varieties, are all fairly scarce.

BIBLIOGRAPHY

Goodacre, Hugh. *A Handbook of the Coinage of the Byzantine Empire,* London, 1964 (reprint), p. 125.

Sear, David R. *Byzantine Coins and Their Values,* London, 1987, pp. 276-278.

Wroth, W. *Imperial Byzantine Coins in the British Museum,* reprint, Chicago, 1966, pp. xxxiv, xxxv.

Anastasius II, AD 713-715
AV solidus (x1.5)
Constantinople mint

MINTS

Sardinia
Syracuse
Catania
Naples
Rome
Ravenna
Constantinople

The secretary of Philippicus, a civil servant by the name Artemius, was named by the Senate to replace the deposed Philippicus on the throne. Although history records this accession as an accidental one, it is difficult to believe that there was not some acquiescence of the powers in Constantinople to the removal of Philippicus.

Artemius chose the name Anastasius at his coronation, in remembrance of the civil servant by that same name who had earlier served the empire long and well.

Like the coins of his predecessor, those of Anastasius II are scarce or rare in virtually all cases. This is remarkable, considering the number of mints at which they were struck—three more than his predecessor. There are several cases of shorter reigns producing coins which have survived in much greater quantities. The most readily available coins of Anastasius II seem to be the bronzes from Constantinople, although the solidi do appear at auction from time to time. Two unique silver coins, a 1/8 siliqua (30 nummi) from Rome, and a hexagram from Constantinople (struck from solidus dies) are known for this reign. Anastasius II was displaced by another revolt of malcontent troops from the Opsikion theme.

BIBLIOGRAPHY

Fairhead, N. "A Catanian Follis of Anastasius II", *Numismatic Circular*, 88:12, 1980, pp. 444-45.

O'Hara, M.D. and I. Vecchi. "A find of Byzantine Silver from the Mint of Rome for the period A.D. 641-752", *Swiss Numismatic Review*, 64, 1985, pp. 105-140.

Protonotarios, P. "A Semissis of the Emperor Artemius Anastasius", *Numismatic Circular*, 79:10, 1971, p. 363.

ꞮN thЄOꞨOSIꝊS MꝊL

Theodosius was a tax collector at Adramytium when the troops rebelling against Anastasius II proclaimed him emperor. It is impossible to believe that this is all that there is to the story, but the chroniclers are silent.

The only facts which we know with certainty are that Anastasius was indeed overthrown by a military coup, and that he escaped with his life, and surprisingly with his nose intact. Apparently the episode with Justinian's second reign made it clear that nose-slitting was not only barbaric, but ineffective as a means of dispatching potential claimants to the throne.

Theodosius III was not accepted in the provinces as sovereign, and it was inevitable that there should be a movement against him. When Leo the "Isaurian" moved against Constantinople, Theodosius wisely abdicated the throne and retired back to private life (Ostrogorsky has him retiring to a monastery in Ephesus). This incredible episode is one of the very few cases in which an emperor was able to walk away from the purple without being avenged, mutilated or exiled. The fact that he had no military power base or broad ambitions undoubtedly preserved his life and freedom.

Theodosius III, AD 715-717
AV solidus (x1.5)
Constantinople mint

MINTS
Sardinia
Syracuse
Naples
Rome
Ravenna
Constantinople

BIBLIOGRAPHY

Goodacre, Hugh. *A Handbook of the Coinage of the Byzantine Empire*, London, 1964 (reprint), pp. 129-130.

Ostrogorsky, George. *History of the Byzantine State*, Rutgers, 1957, pp. 154-156.

Vasiliev, A.A. *History of the Byzantine Empire, 324-1453*, Univ. of Wisconsin, 1952, p. 229.

The Isaurian Dynasty

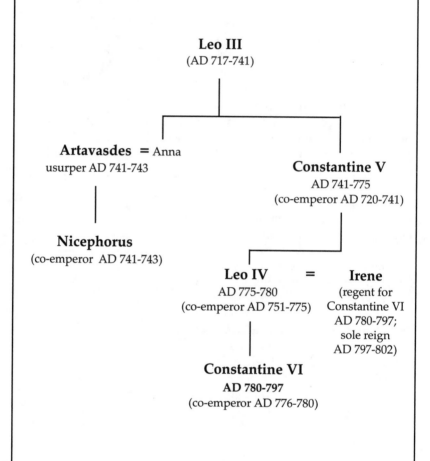

Leo III
(AD 717-741)

Artavasdes = Anna
usurper AD 741-743

Nicephorus
(co-emperor AD 741-743)

Constantine V
AD 741-775
(co-emperor AD 720-741)

Leo IV   =   **Irene**
AD 775-780   (regent for
(co-emperor AD 751-775)   Constantine VI
AD 780-797;
sole reign
AD 797-802)

Constantine VI
AD 780-797
(co-emperor AD 776-780)

ꝊNO LꞰON P A MꜹL

Leo had been placed in charge of the Anatolikon theme by Anastasius Artemius. He was a native of Germanicea in Commagene (not from Isauria) and a very able general, who came to the throne in response to the vacuum of power in Constantinople at the time. In 720, he associated his young son Constantine V with him as co-emperor.

Leo's reign is seen by historians as a critical juncture, at which the future of Europe was in the balance. The Muslim expansion had reached the walls of Constantinople and all that stood between them and Europe was the city itself. At the time, Europe could not have withstood the onslaught. His crushing defeat of the Arabs at the siege of Constantinople preserved the security of the empire and of Europe itself.

The other great event of Leo's reign was the proclamation forbidding the veneration of icons—which initiated the Iconoclastic controversy that raged for the next century. This brought him into bitter conflict with the church and greatly undermined his popularity among the people.

Leo III, AD 717-741
AV solidus (x1.5), Constantinople

Constantine V, AD 720-741
co-emperor (reverse of above)

MINTS
Sardinia
Syracuse
Rome
uncertain Italy
Constantinople

BIBLIOGRAPHY

Diehl, C. "Leo III and the Isaurian Dynasty (717-802), *The Cambridge Medieval History* IV, 1923, pp. 1-26.

Grierson, P. "A New Early Follis Type of Leo III (718)", *Numismatic Chronicle*, 1974, pp. 75-77.

___. "The copper coinage of Leo III (717-41) and Constantine V (720-75)", *Numismatic Chronicle, 1965*, pp. 183-196.

Weller, H. "X-N on the Iconoclast's Copper Coinage", *Numismatic Circular*, 84:4, 1976, pp. 144-145.

G APtAЧASDOS MЧLt / G NIChFORЧS MЧLtЧA

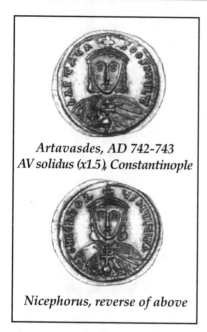

Artavasdes, AD 742-743
AV solidus (x1.5), Constantinople

Nicephorus, reverse of above

MINTS
Constantinople
Rome

Like Leo in Anatolia, Artavasdes had been appointed Strategus of the Armeniakon theme by Anastasius II. He was married to Anna, the daughter of Leo III and sister of Constantine V. Sometime between 741 and 744 (historians disagree on the precise dates) he overthrew his brother-in-law Constantine and was proclaimed emperor. Constantine fled to Asia Minor. Artavasdes immediately associated his son Nicephorus with him as co-emperor and they appear together on coins.

Artavasdes was an iconodule and restored the icons to the great satisfaction of the church and the people. From exile, Constantine was able to reorganize his army in Asia Minor and met Artavasdes at Sardes in 743—where he prevailed and was reinstalled on the throne. In retribution, Artavasdes and Nicephorus were publicly blinded in the Hippodrome, and their supporters were mutilated in the same spectacle. The Patriarch was led around the Hippodrome on an ass in humiliation.

The coins of Artavasdes are among the rarest in this series. One specimen in Paris, which keeps appearing in the literature (Wroth p. 392; Goodacre p. 145; Sear p. 294) is a strange coin, usually regarded as a die-engraver's error, with Artavasdes on the obverse and Constantine V on the reverse—an incongruous match to be sure.

BIBLIOGRAPHY

Boyce, Aline A. "A Solidus of Artavasdes", *ANSMN V,* 1952, pp. 89-102.
Ostrogorsky, George. *History of the Byzantine State,* Rutgers, 1957, pp. 165-166.

G N CONSTANTINυS

Copronymus, the son of Leo III was a good soldier and politician. He also was an iconoclast, like his father, and continued the prohibitions. Despite successes against the Muslims, Bulgars and Slavs, Ravenna was lost to the Lombards in 751—the same year that Constantine's son, Leo IV, was made co-emperor. By 763, the borders had been secured and Constantine entered the capital in a classical Roman Triumph.

The Lombards, in turn, were defeated by Charlemagne in 771. This resulted in a fundamental and permanent change in the West.

Although his reign was interrupted by the usurpation of Artavasdes, Constantine managed to keep fairly tight control of the empire. He sponsored the restoration of several public works, but his popularity was tarnished by the intense persecution of iconodules. He apparently was not mourned greatly when he died on campaign in 775.

The coinage of Constantine V, especially the bronze, is fairly common. It is popular, however, because there are several imperial portrait varieties.

Constantine V, AD 741-775
AV solidus (x1.5)
Constantinople mint

Constantine V & Leo IV,
AV solidus, AD 751-775
rev: posthumous Leo III

MINTS
Syracuse
Rome
Ravenna
Constantinople

BIBLIOGRAPHY

Grierson, P. "The copper coinage of Leo III (717-41) and Constantine V (720-75)", *Numismatic Chronicle*, 1965, pp. 183-196.

Lombard, A. *Constantin V, empereur des Romains (740-775)*, Paris, 1902.

Wroth, W. *Imperial Byzantine Coins in the British Museum*, reprint, Chicago, 1966, pp. xxxvii and 378-390.

Leo IV, the Khazar
ΛΕΟΝ VS S ΕϤϤΟΝ CONSTANTINOS O NEOS

Leo IV, AD 751-780
AV semissis (x1.75)
Syracuse mint

MINTS
Syracuse
Rome
Constantinople

Leo IV, the son of Constantine V, was called "the Khazar" because his mother was a Khazar princess. He ruled jointly with his father from 751 and as senior Augustus from 775 to 780.

Leo was married to a beautiful Athenian girl named Irene who bore him a son. He associated this son, Constantine VI, with him as co-emperor in 776. Irene was opposed to the persecution of Iconodules, if not one herself, and during Leo's reign the persecutions were at least moderated. The prohibitions were not lifted however. He also ended the persecution of the monastic order which had suffered under his father.

The reverse of one series of coins issued by Leo IV depicts his father, and grandfather (Leo III) who are identified in the legend. On the obverse of these coins are the portraits of Leo IV and Constantine VI. This is a wonderful family tree of four generations and a very popular dynastic coin.

Leo was always in fragile health, and following a vigorous campaign against the Arabs, he died prematurely—after a sole reign of only five years.

BIBLIOGRAPHY

Goodacre, Hugh. *A Handbook of the Coinage of the Byzantine Empire*, London, 1964 (reprint), pp. 146-148.

Metcalf. D.M. "How extensive was the issue of folles during the years 775-820?, *Byzantion*, xxxvi, 1967, pp. 288-295.

Sear, David R. *Byzantine Coins and Their Values*, London, 1987, pp. 301-302.

Vasiliev, A.A. *History of the Byzantine Empire, 324-1453*, Univ. of Wisconsin, 1952, p. 263.

Whitting, P.D. *Byzantine Coins*, London, 1973, p. 167.

Constantine VI and Irene
CONStANtINOS CA b′ Δ′

Because Constantine VI was a minor when his father died, the empire was placed in the hands of his mother, Irene, as regent.

At about the age of twenty (AD 790), Constantine tried to break loose from his mother and assume his rightful position as basileus. He was encouraged by supporters of Iconoclasm who were loathe to see Irene lift the prohibitions. Irene was deposed and her advisers were discharged. However, in less than two years she was reinstated in her old position as a co-ruler.

The joint, but far from happy, reign of mother and son lasted until 797. During this period, Irene did everything possible to enhance her own prestige and image, while portraying her son as unfit to rule. He had not acquitted himself well during the Bulgarian War of 792, and was becoming increasingly reckless and cruel. A rebellion by his uncle, Nicephorus, was squelched and Constantine showed little mercy. He blinded the perpetrator and cut off the tongues of his father's four surviving brothers. This played right into the hand of Irene, who sought only to rid herself of his interference and rule alone. He divorced his wife Maria and married his mistress, named Theodote, crowning her as empress. This set him at odds with the church and the people alike.

By 797 he had alienated all of his supporters and Irene was able to move against him without opposition. In the Purple Room of the palace, where he was born, Constantine was blinded and deposed.

Constantine VI & Irene
AD 780-797, AV solidus
(x1.5)Constantinople mint

MINTS
Constantinople

BIBLIOGRAPHY

Ostrogorsky, George. *History of the Byzantine State*, Rutgers, 1957, pp. 177-181.

Wroth, W. *Imperial Byzantine Coins in the British Museum*, reprint, Chicago, 1966, pp. xxxviii-xl and 397-399.

ЄIRIΠH bASILISSH

Irene, AD 797-802
AV solidus (x1.5)
Constantinople mint

MINTS
Syracuse
Constantinople

The beauty of Irene is evident in the effigy that we find on her coins. Even though the style of the day precluded emphasis of physical features, it is clear that this was not a woman wanting of charm. Unfortunately, her charm masked diabolical ambition.

Having deposed her son Constantine VI in 797, she ruled alone from that time until 802. She was the first woman ever to rule the empire in her own name as a sovereign. There were even negotiations for her and Charlemagne to be united in marriage, which would have been a mega-merger to be sure.

Beauty, ambition and cunning were not enough, however, to manage the affairs of state. The court of Irene was one filled with intrigue and internal fighting. In order to maintain the favor of the people she remitted heavy taxes and import/export duties at a time when the imperial treasury was not able to support the losses. She also built many convents and established charities, while putting on an ostentatious display at every public occasion. The resulting financial ruin led to even greater problems.

Irene was eventually deposed by her treasurer, Nicephorus, and banished to Lesbos where she died in abject poverty. She was buried at one of the island convents she had founded in the Sea of Marmora.

BIBLIOGRAPHY

Bury, J.B. "Charles the Great and Irene", *Hermathena*, VIII, 1893, pp. 17-37.
Goodacre, Hugh. *A Handbook of the Coinage of the Byzantine Empire*, London, 1964 (reprint), pp. 154-155.
Jenkins, R. Byzantium: *The Imperial Centuries*, New York, 1966, pp. 90-104 (Chapter on Constantine VI and Irene)
Vasiliev, A.A. *History of the Byzantine Empire, 324-1453*, Univ. of Wisconsin, 1952, p. 263-269.

Nicephorus I (Logothete) and Stauracius
ПICIFOROS bASILE' / StAVRACIS ꞜЄSPO' X

Nicephorus, Irene's treasurer, led a palace insurrection to have himself installed as emperor. There are very few sources for his reign, the primary one being Theophanes. He was obviously a man of sound financial ability and quickly put the empire back on sound footing with new tribute levies and taxes—even on the church. About a year later he raised his son Stauracius to the rank of co-emperor. In 803 Nicephorus concluded a temporary treaty with Charlemagne which defined the limits of the Eastern and Western Roman Empires. The latter had been crowned emperor in 800 by the Pope at Rome.

Nicephorus I, AD 802-811
AV solidus, Constantinople
Stauracius on reverse

MINTS
Syracuse
Naples
Constantinople

In 809 the caliph Harun ar-Rashid died, leaving the Muslims in disarray. This temporarily removed the threat on the empire's eastern frontiers, allowing Nicephorus to deal with the Bulgars. Under the leadership of Krum, they had become a serious threat to the north. Nicephorus personally led his army into the field and won an important battle against Krum at Pliska. Flushed with victory, they pursued the Bulgars into the hill country—which proved to be a fatal mistake. The Romans were ambushed and Nicephorus became the first emperor to die in battle in over 400 years.

Stauracius too was mortally wounded in this action, but was able to make his way back to Constantinople. There, in his last days, he relinquished the empire to his brother-in-law, Michael I Rhangabe.

BIBLIOGRAPHY

Bury, J.B. *A History of the Eastern Roman Empire from the Fall of Irene to the Accession of Basil I (A.D.802-867)*, London, 1912.

Jenkins, R. Byzantium: *The Imperial Centuries*, New York, 1966, pp. 117-129 (Chapter on Nicephorus I and Michael I)

Wroth, W. *Imperial Byzantine Coins in the British Museum*, reprint, Chicago, 1966, pp. xl and 401-404.

Michael I and Theophylactus
AD 811-813, AE follis (x1.5)
Constantinople

MINTS

Syracuse
Constantinople

Michael Rhangabe was apparently a Slav who married Procopia, the daughter of Nicephorus I and sister of Stauracius. He campaigned with his father-in-law in the fateful encounter that took the life of the emperor and mortally wounded his successor. Rhangabe returned to Constantinople with the dying Stauracius, and shortly thereafter was crowned emperor. He elevated his son Theophylactus to the rank of co-emperor within a few months.

The reign of Michael was short and disastrous. On a positive note, he finally concluded the peace negotiations with Charlemagne that had been underway for twelve years. On the Bulgarian front things were a complete fiasco. Thrace and Macedonia were completely exposed to the Bulgar Khan and poor diplomacy merely aggravated the situation as Krum was quick to avenge the slightest insult. Finally, Michael met Krum with a force large enough to take the day. Instead of taking the advantage, he dallied for days until the impatient generals insisted on an attack. Giving in he did so, but the Asian troops under his command fled the field and left the rest of the army exposed. The result was devastating.

The troops then proclaimed Leo the Armenian emperor and advanced on Constantinople. Michael was deposed and exiled along with his entire family.

BIBLIOGRAPHY

Goodacre, Hugh. *A Handbook of the Coinage of the Byzantine Empire,* London, 1964 (reprint), pp. 161-163.
Sear, David R. *Byzantine Coins and Their Values,* London, 1987, pp. 309-310.
Vasiliev, A.A. *History of the Byzantine Empire, 324-1453,* Univ. of Wisconsin, 1952, p. 271.

Leo V and Constantine
LEON bASILEY' / CONSTANT' ⱰESPX

Leo was the son of Bardas, the Armenian, and was commander of imperial forces in Armenia when Michael I was defeated by the Bulgarians at Versinikia. During that battle, forces loyal to Leo deserted Michael—causing the battle to be lost—and Leo was acclaimed emperor. He associated his son Constantine with him as co-emperor on Christmas day of 813—a portentous day for the family.

He was a skilled general, and managed to repel the Bulgars when they made their inevitable assault on Constantinople. In 815, Krum died and Leo concluded a 30 year peace with the new Khan.

Leo V and Constantine
AV solidus, AD 813-820
Constantinople

MINTS
Syracuse
Constantinople

He held strong Iconoclastic views and tried to reassert the policies which had faded somewhat by that time. In the Council of 815 the prohibitions against icons was restored and images were ordered removed. It proved to be an unpopular move, leading to Leo's assassination in Hagia Sophia on Christmas day of 820. The successor, Constantine, and his brothers were mutilated as the traditional means of disqualification for imperial office. They, along with their sisters and mother Theodosia, were banished to an island. According to one account, the remains of Leo were placed in a sack and thrown into the boat with them.

Michael, the Amorian, was proclaimed the new emperor, inaugurating the reign of another dynasty.

BIBLIOGRAPHY

Jenkins, R. Byzantium: *The Imperial Centuries*, New York, 1966, pp. 130-139 (Chapter on Leo V and the Iconoclast revival)
Ostrogorsky, George. *History of the Byzantine State*, Rutgers, 1957, pp. 200-203.
Wroth, W. *Imperial Byzantine Coins in the British Museum*, reprint, Chicago, 1966, pp. xli and 409-413.

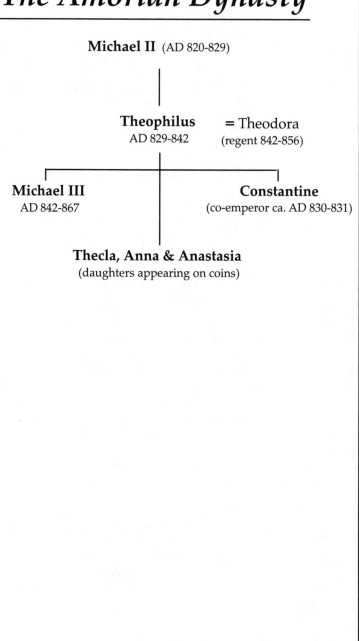

The Amorian Dynasty

Michael II (AD 820-829)

Theophilus   = Theodora
AD 829-842   (regent 842-856)

Michael III   **Constantine**
AD 842-867   (co-emperor ca. AD 830-831)

Thecla, Anna & Anastasia
(daughters appearing on coins)

Michael II, the Amorian
MIXAHL bASILE'

Michael came from Amorium in Phrygia (north central Turkey) and made his way to prominence in the military. He was a peasant soldier and took pride in his knowledge of nature and living things. He spoke Greek with a lisp and was nicknamed Michael the Lisper. Shortly after his accession, Michael raised his son Theophilus to the rank of co-emperor.

Early in their reign, Michael and Theophilus were besieged at Constantinople by Thomas the Slav, a former comrade from service in Anatolia. Leo V, Michael II and Thomas had together visited a seer at Philomelium, who said that two of them would someday become emperors. Thomas should have heeded those words, since Leo and Michael had each ascended the throne already. His siege lasted over a year, but ended in his capture and execution.

Michael II, AD 820-829
AV solidus (x2)
Constantinople mint

MINTS
Syracuse
Constantinople

This siege left the East exposed, and the Arabs were on the advance once again toward the end of Michael's reign. Crete was lost and Sicily was under heavy attack. Michael II died in 829, apparently of kidney disease, and was the first emperor in a half century to die peacefully as the head of state. He left a healthy son, Theophilus, who carried on the dynasty his father had founded.

BIBLIOGRAPHY

Bendall, Simon. "Miliaresia of the Reign of Michael II", *Numismatic Circular*, 91:2, 1983, p. 44.

Jenkins, R. Byzantium: *The Imperial Centuries*, New York, 1966, pp. 140-152 (Chapter on Michael II and Theophilus)

Metcalf, D.M. "The folles of Michael II and of Theophilus before his reform", *Hamburger Beiträge zur Numismatik* , 7:21(1967), pp. 21-34.

Vasiliev, A. *Byzance et les Arabes. I. La dynastie d'Amorium (820-867)*, Brussels, 1935.

ϴΕOFILOS bASILE'

Theophilus, AD 829-842
AV solidus (x1.5), Constantinople

Constantine, ca. AD 830-831
AV solidus (x1.75)
Constantinople mint

MINTS

Syracuse
Naples
Constantinople

Theophilus was raised to the rank of co-emperor and married to Theodora on the same day—the 12th of May 821. He was a staunch iconoclast, and the historians have accordingly treated him with some contempt. It should be remembered that nearly all history of this period is ecclesiastical history and subject to severe bias. He was well educated, and a patron of the arts, with a sense of justice and compassion. Theophilus was one of the few emperors that was accessible to the common man and even frequented local markets.

Militarily, the empire was troubled during this reign. Even the dynasty's ancestral homeland of Amorium was lost to the Arabs amidst a terrible slaughter of its citizens. Sicily also continued to slip away.

Constantine was the eldest son of Theophilus and Theodora. He was elevated to the throne as co-emperor shortly after his father's accession, but apparently died within a year or so. Their infant son Michael was named co-emperor in September, 840.

BIBLIOGRAPHY

Bellinger, A.R. "The Emperor Theophilus and the Lagbe Hoard", *Berytus,* VIII, 1943-44, pp. 102-106.

Dikigoropoulos, A. "The Constantinopolitan solidi of Theophilus", *Dumbarton Oaks Papers,* 18, 1964, pp. 353-361.

Metcalf, D.M. "The reformed folles of Theophilus: their styles and localization", *ANSMN* 14, 1968, pp. 121-153.

___. The new bronze coinage of Theophilus and the growth of the Balkan themes", *ANSMN* 10, 1961, pp. 81-98.

MIXAHL bASILϵ'

When Theophilus died in 842, Michael was only two years old. His older brother Constantine had died prematurely and the regency was assumed by Michael's mother Theodora and his older sister Thecla. Although only three years old when it happened, the most notable event of his reign was the synod at which iconoclasm was finally condemned.

In 856, at the age of sixteen, Michael conspired with Bardas—the brother of Theodora—to remove his mother from authority and claim the throne on his own. He relied heavily on his court to conduct the affairs of state and took on a playboy lifestyle. His favorite amusement was the horse races. In the year 864, the Bulgar Khan Boris was baptized as an Orthodox Christian, reducing tensions on the northern frontier. In 866 Michael elevated Basil, a Macedonian of peasant origin, to the rank of co-emperor. It was a costly mistake, as Basil murdered his benefactor on the 23rd of September, 867.

Michael III alone,
AD 856-866, AV solidus (x1.5)

Michael III & Theodora,
AD 842-856, AV solidus (x1.5)

Michael III & Thecla
AV solidus (x1.5)

MINTS
Syracuse
Constantinople
Cherson

BIBLIOGRAPHY

Carlton, Walker. "A Gold Solidus of the Byzantine Emperor Michael III Marks the End of Iconoclasm", *SAN*, 18:3, 1992, pp. 67ff.

Portner, A.. "A Sicilian Tremissis of Michael III", *Numismatic Circular*, 89:9, 1981, p.277.

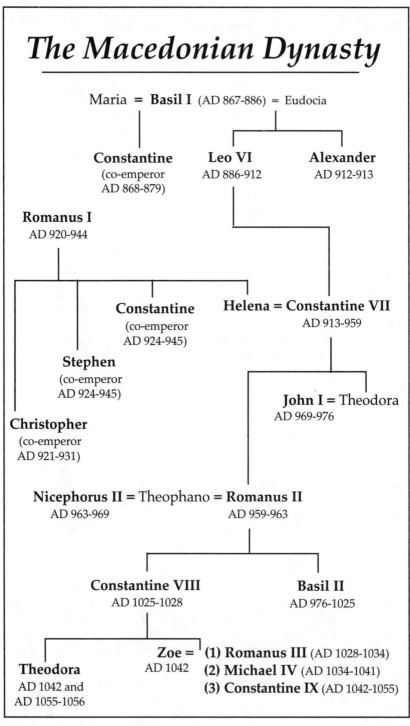

The Macedonian Dynasty

Maria = **Basil I** (AD 867-886) = Eudocia

Constantine
(co-emperor
AD 868-879)

Leo VI
AD 886-912

Alexander
AD 912-913

Romanus I
AD 920-944

Constantine
(co-emperor
AD 924-945)

Helena = Constantine VII
AD 913-959

Stephen
(co-emperor
AD 924-945)

John I = Theodora
AD 969-976

Christopher
(co-emperor
AD 921-931)

Nicephorus II = Theophano = **Romanus II**
AD 963-969   AD 959-963

Constantine VIII
AD 1025-1028

Basil II
AD 976-1025

Theodora
AD 1042 and
AD 1055-1056

Zoe =
AD 1042

(1) Romanus III (AD 1028-1034)
(2) Michael IV (AD 1034-1041)
(3) Constantine IX (AD 1042-1055)

Basil the Macedonian did not seize power by attacking the capital with a rebellious army, he merely murdered his associate. In fairness, it may have been a matter of self preservation. Regardless, Basil turned out to be a strong and effective ruler. He greatly expanded the empire by recovering lands lost during earlier reigns—especially in the West. In the East he advanced as far as Mesopotamia. His other great achievement was the formulation of the legal codes which were published by Leo VI in his name.

That his rule must have been evenhanded is attested to by the fact that the Amorian Dynasty could not mount an effective effort to recover its throne. Basil's son Constantine (by his first wife, Maria) was elevated to co-emperor in 868 and his son Leo VI, (by the second wife, Eudocia) in 870. Constantine died unexpectedly in 879, and Leo's brother Alexander was then elevated in his place.

Basil was killed in a hunting accident in 886 and Leo VI assumed his father's throne as senior emperor.

Basil I, AD 867-886
AV semissis (x2), Syracuse mint

Basil I, Constantine and Leo VI
AE follis, Constantinople

MINTS

Syracuse
Constantinople
Cherson
uncertain provincial

BIBLIOGRAPHY

Jenkins, R. Byzantium: *The Imperial Centuries,* New York, 1966, pp. 183-197 (Chapter on Basil the Macedonian).

Metcalf, D.M. "The Antalya hoard of miliaresia of Basil I", *Numismatic Chronicle,* 1977, pp. 114-125.

___. "Razba follu Basilia La organizace jejích mincoven [The follis coinage of Basil I and the organization of the mints]", *Numismatick´y Sborník* 9, Prague, 1966, pp. 95-127. (In Czech, with English summary and 5 plates).

Leo VI, the Wise
LΣON bASILΣVS ROM

Leo VI, AD 886-912
AV solidus (x1.75)
Constantinople mint

MINTS
Constantinople
Cherson
uncertain provincial

Leo, nicknamed "The Wise" was a studious person, quite unlike his father—but for their common interest in the law. He finished the work begun by Basil which established a new legal code for the empire. The codex was named *Basilica* in honor of his father. Much of the land reclaimed by Basil was once again lost, as Leo showed little interest in foreign relations. Alexander, Leo's brother, was associated with him as co-emperor throughout the reign, but did not take an active part in government either. Leo finally fathered an heir in 905 and named him Constantine (VII).

An interesting aspect of the coinage of Leo is that on certain issues he is portrayed seated on a distinctive lyre-backed throne. This same throne appears on a famous mosaic which still may be seen in the Narthex of Hagia Sophia (see page 29). The identity of the prostrate emperor in the mosaic is a matter of some debate, but that is really not the issue here. In that mosaic scene, Christ occupies the same imperial throne as Leo. This not-so-subtle visual metaphor is but one stage in the ever-increasing representation of the emperor as a manifestation of Christ on earth.

BIBLIOGRAPHY

Cutler, A. "The Lyre-backed throne", *Transfigurations: Studies in the Dynamics of Byzantine Iconography*, Penn State Press, 1975.

Goodacre, Hugh. *A Handbook of the Coinage of the Byzantine Empire*, London, 1964 (reprint), pp. 190-194.

Jenkins, R. Byzantium: *The Imperial Centuries*, New York, 1966, pp. 198-211 (Chapter on Leo the Wise).

Oikonomides, N. "Leo VI and the Narthex Mosaic of Saint Sophia", *Dumbarton Oaks Papers*, 1976, pp. 153-72.

ALEXANdROS AyGystOS ROM

Alexander was the younger brother of Leo VI and was elevated to the throne as co-emperor in 879 under Basil I. He was associated with Leo throughout his entire reign and came to power on his own when Leo died leaving only a seven-year-old son (Constantine VII). Alexander seems to have been an insolent and vindictive ruler with a very short temper. He paid little heed to his brother's advisors and brought turmoil to both domestic and foreign affairs. In a fit of belligerency, he withheld the annual tribute to the Bulgars and brought the wrath of that tribe upon the empire—a disastrous consequence. He was extremely unpopular as a ruler, and was sure to be deposed, but during a game of ball he suffered a cerebral hemorrhage and died two days later—saving his adversaries the effort of removing him.

Alexander, AD 912-913
AV solidus (x1.75)
(being crowned by his patron Saint Alexander)
Constantinople mint

MINTS
Constantinople
Cherson

This circumstance led to a bitter confrontation between the Patriarch Nicholas and the mother of Constantine VII over his regency. At first, the Patriarch prevailed but within a year Zoe was invited back by the chief magister to assume the regency of her son.

BIBLIOGRAPHY

Jenkins, R. Byzantium: *The Imperial Centuries,* New York, 1966, pp. 227-240 (Chapter on Alexander and the Regency, 912-920).

Musmov, N.A. "Une monnais d'argent de l'empereur Alexandre", *Byzantion,* VI (1931), pp. 99-100.

Wroth, W. *Imperial Byzantine Coins in the British Museum,* reprint, Chicago, 1966, pp. xlvii and 450.

+constant bASIL ROM

Constantine VII
AV solidus (x1.5), AD 908-959
Constantinople mint

Constantine VII and Zoe
AE follis, AD 913-919

MINTS
Constantinople
Cherson

Constantine VII was Augustus for 51 years—being associated with Leo VI, The Patriarch Nicholas, Zoe, Alexander, Romanus I, Christopher, Stephen, Constantine and Romanus II. He was elevated to the rank of co-emperor by his father and, although still a minor, continued as such during the reign of Alexander—his father's brother. When Alexander died, Constantine came under the regency of Nicholas and then of his mother, Zoe.

He was a scholarly person with little interest in affairs of state. Fortunately, his disposition toward writing left us with *De ceremoniis* (The Book of Ceremonies)—one of the most insightful sources available on court life and practice in the 9th and 10th centuries. Constantine is often referred to as the guiding spirit of the "Macedonian Renaissance".

BIBLIOGRAPHY

Bury, J.B. "The Ceremonial Book of Constantine Porphyrogennetos", *English Historical Review* 22, April 1907, pp. 209-227 and July 1907, pp. 417-39.

Gregory, Timothy E. "The gold coinage of the Emperor Constantine VII, *ANSMN* 19, 1974, pp. 87-118.

Lis, L.J. "The coins of Constantine VII reflect political changes in the empire", *The Celator*, 11:09, September 1997, pp. 36-38.

Matthews, Jane Timken. "The Source for the Solidus Issued by Constantine VII in 945", *ANSMN* 24, 1979, pp. 199-212.

+RⱣMAꞀ bASILⱢVS RⱣM

Lecapenus was the family name of an able general who was called upon to manage the empire in the face of serious external problems. Constantine VII's first regent, the Patriarch Nicholas, had concluded an agreement with the Bulgar Khan Symeon which amounted to an elevation as co-emperor. As soon as the Bulgar withdrew from Constantinople there was a palace uprising that displaced the Patriarch. The new regent, Zoe, was not equipped to deal with Symeon who retaliated with a vengeance. Therefore, Romanus was brought in as regent and Constantine was married to his daughter.

Constantine's new father-in-law was raised to the rank of co-emperor a year later, and by 924 had raised his three sons—Christopher, Stephen and Constantine—as associates as well. After many years in power, two of the sons of Romanus conspired and succeeded in overthrowing him. They were immediately routed by Constantine VII who found himself the sole ruler for the first time in his life.

Romanus I, AD 920-944
AE follis (x1.5), Constantinople

Romanus I & Christopher
AD 921-931. AV solidus (x1.5)

MINTS
Constantinople
Cherson

BIBLIOGRAPHY

Jenkins, R. Byzantium: *The Imperial Centuries*, New York, 1966, pp. 241-255 (Chapter on Romanus I).

Runciman, S. *The Emperor Romanus Lecapenus and his reign*, Cambridge, 1929.

Wroth, W. *Imperial Byzantine Coins in the British Museum*, reprint, Chicago, 1966, pp. xlviii-xlix and 453-459.

ROMAN AVtOCRAt' ROM

Constantine VII & Romanus II,
AD 945-959, Constantinople
(Romanus II reigned
alone from AD 959-963)

MINTS
Constantinople

Following the family revolt which displaced Romanus Lecapenus, and subsequently his sons, Constantine VII raised his six-year-old son Romanus II to the rank of co-emperor. The boy had the benefit of 14 years as understudy for the role of senior augustus, but it did not seem to be enough as he was not a great leader or head of state.

Fortunately, he inherited a prosperous empire with an army led by great generals. Further adding to the imperial resources, Nicephorus Phocas recaptured Crete, Cilicia, Antioch and Aleppo from the Arabs during this reign.

In 956 Romanus II married Theophano, the daughter of an innkeeper, who was apparently beautiful and ambitious. Although he died at the tender age of 24, Romanus II left two sons—Basil II, whom he had crowned in 960 and Constantine VIII, who was named to share the throne in 961. It was rumored that Theophano had poisoned her husband and she came at odds immediately with Joseph Bringas, the new regent for her son. It was a replay of the old scenario with Zoe and Patriarch Nicholas. Theophano went to the general Nicephorus for aid and Bringas was ousted. Nicephorus was proclaimed emperor by his troops, then married Theophano to become stepfather of the legitimate emperor Basil II—whom he essentially ignored from that point on.

BIBLIOGRAPHY

Grierson, P. *Byzantine Coins,* Berkeley, 1982, pp. 170-180. (Includes an overview of the Early Macedonian Dynasty to AD 969.)

Jenkins, R. Byzantium: *The Imperial Centuries,* New York, 1966, pp. 269-283 (Chapter on Romanus II and Nicephorus II).

Whitting, P.D. *Byzantine Coins,* London, 1973, p. 190.

+ΠICIFR bASIL ROM

Before Nicephorus married Theophano, she was still technically regent for Basil II, but we do not find any coins in her name. The unique bronze coin published in Wroth as Theophano (now lost) seems to have been either a forgery or a seal. Officially ignoring her, Nicephorus accepted her children only nominally.

His military achievements continued to grow and public works were undertaken during the six years that he was in power. At this time, the great monastery on Mt. Athos was built. The burden of constant military ventures, successful or not, caused a strain on the population and Nicephorus became unpopular at home.

Theophano, perhaps in the hope of restoring her sons to power, conspired with John Tzimisces, a nephew of Nicephorus, and had the emperor murdered. Tzimisces, to secure his own coronation, cast the guilt on Theophano and she was subsequently exiled.

Nicephorus II, AD 963-969
AV histamenon nomisma (x1.5)
Constantinople mint

Nicephorus II & Basil II
AD 963-969, AV histamenon (x1.5)
Constantinople mint

MINTS

Constantinople
Cherson

BIBLIOGRAPHY

Ahrweiler-Glykatzi, H. "Nouvelle hypothèse sur le tétartèron d'or de la politique monétaire de Nicéphore Phocas", *Mélanges Georges Ostrogorsky I*, pp. 1-9, Belgrade, 1963.

O'Hara, M.D. "A follis of Nicephorus II Phocas", *Seaby Coin and Medal Bulletin*, 1973, pp. 120-123.

Schlumberger, G. *Un empereur byzantine au Xe siècle: Nicéphore Phocas*, Paris, 1890, 2nd ed. 1923.

Wroth, W. *Imperial Byzantine Coins in the British Museum*, reprint, Chicago, 1966, pp. xlix-l and 470-473.

John I, AD 969-976
AR miliaresion (x1.5)
Constantinople mint

MINTS
Constantinople
Cherson

Having ascended the throne under a dark cloud, John set out to bolster his legitimacy by taking the hand of a daughter of Constantine VII. The fact that she had taken the vows of a nun did not seem to bother, as she was easily absolved and became Theodora the empress instead.

In 972, relations between East and West were improved when the princess Theophano was married to Otto II, the future emperor of Germany. She was either a sister to the two young sons of Romanus, or a relative of Tzimisces—the sources are not clear. Basil II and Constantine VIII were still co-emperors, at least in name, but their names did not appear on coins struck under Tzimisces.

John was a brilliant general, like his murdered uncle, and completely routed the Russians who had advanced into Bulgaria and were threatening the city of Constantinople. He then marched East into Syria and conducted a series of campaigns which struck fear into the Muslims and netted the empire some three million nomisma in tribute and ransoms—some of which was restruck into imperial coinage. This vigorous campaigning took its toll on Tzimisces and he died in 976 of natural causes.

Basil II and Constantine VIII were finally on the throne in their own right, although there were still a host of contenders for the purple.

BIBLIOGRAPHY

Goodacre, Hugh. *A Handbook of the Coinage of the Byzantine Empire*, London, 1964 (reprint), pp. 211-214.
Ostrogorsky, George. *History of the Byzantine State*, Rutgers, 1957, pp. 293-298.
Vasiliev, A.A. *History of the Byzantine Empire, 324-1453*, Univ. of Wisconsin, 1952, pp. 310-311.

Basil II, Bulgaroctonos
+bASIL' C constant' b R

Basil II was acknowledged as senior augustus on January 10, 976. Although he had been in the shadows for a long time, he still was only 18 years old. Nevertheless, Basil was a born leader and he took the empire to new heights in his reign of nearly half a century. Constantine VIII, his younger brother, was inclined to revel in the luxury of his station and this apparently suited Basil.

In 980, Basil received a gift from Vladimir of Russia consisting of some 6,000 Scandinavian/Russian troops. These became known as the Varangian Guard and continued to serve the emperors of Constantinople for over 300 years.

The expansion of Samuel in Bulgaria caused great alarm at Constantinople and Basil was obliged to mount a major campaign against the Khan. The name Bulgaroctonos means "Bulgar-slayer" and was an epithet given to Basil in recognition of his decisive victory, which brought all of Bulgaria into the empire in 1018. Basil was active militarily right up to his death in 1025. He is remembered by history as one of the greatest emperors of the medieval period.

Basil II, AD 976-1025
AV histamenon nomisma
Basil (left) and Constantine VIII

MINTS

Constantinople
Cherson

BIBLIOGRAPHY

Dawkins, R.M. "The later history of the Varangian guard", *Journal of Roman Studies*, 37, 1947, pp. 39ff.

Grierson, P. "A Pattern Nomisma of Basil II (976-1025)", *Numismatic Circular*, 85:3, 1977, p. 97.

___. "The gold and silver coinage of Basil II", *ANSMN* 13, 1967, pp. 167-87.

___. "A Misattributed Miliaresion of Basil II", *Mélanges G. Ostrogorsky I*, Belgrade, 1963, pp. 111-116.

Metcalf, D.M. "Byzantine Coins Minted in Central Greece Under Basil II", *Nomismatika Chronika*, 1974, pp. 21-25.

+cѡnstantin bASILEYS ROM

*Constantine VIII, AD 1025-1028
AV histamenon nomisma (x1.5)*

MINTS
Constantinople

According to Michael Psellus, Constantine was 70 years old at the time of his accession as senior emperor. If this were so, it would make him older than Basil II and that can hardly be the case. It is more likely that he was 70, or nearly so, at his death. Although the details are confusing, it is universally agreed that he was a man dedicated to the pursuit of happiness, and that meant of course his own personal happiness. Having inherited a treasury brimming with money from 50 years of taxes, tribute and plunder, he had the means to indulge himself—and did.

Psellus describes him as a man of extraordinary size, with a voracious appetite and a mean temper. Rather than take the field when an uprising occurred on the frontier, Constantine simply paid the quarrelsome barbarians off in cash or titles. Of course the prestige and credibility of the empire suffered greatly. Being rather elderly at his accession, Constantine was afflicted with arthritis and had difficulty walking. Consequently, he chose to ride on horseback everywhere he went. Sensing that he needed an heir, Constantine arranged to have Romanus Argyrus marry his daughter Zoe. Shortly thereafter, he expired following a brief illness and Romanus became emperor.

BIBLIOGRAPHY

Goodacre, Hugh. *A Handbook of the Coinage of the Byzantine Empire*, London, 1964 (reprint), pp. 218-219.

Psellus, Michael. *Fourteen Byzantine Rulers, The Chronographia of Michael Psellus*, English tr. by E.R.A. Sewter, Penguin Books, New York, 1966, pp. 53-59. (Book II on Constantine VIII.)

ΟΣΕ bΟΗΟ' ΡωΜΑΝω

In spite of having achieved a rank of some importance prior to his accession, Romanus had neither the skill nor the energy to be an effective emperor. The successes of his reign were due mainly to the efforts of his military leaders. The one campaign that he led personally was a disaster.

He was a devoted patron of the Virgin Mary, and built a number of churches in her honor. On the reverse of his gold histamena we find a remarkable scene of the emperor being crowned by the Virgin. On silver miliaresia we find a sensitive portrayal of the Virgin Hodegetria, inspired by a famous icon which existed in Constantinople at the time. Seldom can numismatic art of this period be called "sensitive".

Romanus III, AD 1028-1034
AV histamenon nomisma (x1.5)

MINTS
Constantinople

According to some accounts, Zoe tired of her husband because she was barred from access to the imperial treasury and had to live on a fixed allowance. She soon became infatuated with the brother of a court eunuch from Paphlagonia. Zoe was 55 years old at the time—he was much younger. The facts seem to be that Romanus was strangled in his bath on Holy Thursday of 1034 and Zoe married the young Paphlagonian the very same evening. The Patriarch, who had been summoned to perform the marriage, balked at the request. His anxiety was quickly relieved by the donation of 100 pounds of gold. The new emperor was crowned the next day as Michael IV.

BIBLIOGRAPHY

Fagerlie, Joan M. "A miliaresion of Romanus III and a nomisma of Michael IV", *ANSMN* 11, 1964, pp. 227-236.

Jenkins, R. Byzantium: *The Imperial Centuries*, New York, 1966, pp. 339-341.

O'Hara, M.D. "A rare histamenon of Romanus III Argyrus, AD 1028-1034", *Seaby Coin and Medal Bulletin*, 1971, pp. 321-324.

Michael IV, the Paphlagonian
+MIXAHL bASILEYS RM

Michael IV, AD 1034-1041
AV histamenon nomisma (x1.25)
Constantinople mint

MINTS
Constantinople

The real head of state under Michael's reign was apparently his brother, John the Eunuch. Michael was afflicted with epilepsy, as well as dropsy, and it was clear that he would probably not outlive his benefactress. Since there were no heirs, nor likely to be any from the union of Michael and Zoe, John convinced her to adopt their nephew Michael Kalaphates and raise him to the rank of Caesar.

On the frontiers, the general George Maniakes conducted several successful campaigns against the Muslims. However, rebellions in the north resulted in the loss of Serbia and Bulgaria. Michael took to the field himself, in spite of his poor health, and led an army to victory. It was written that he had to be strapped in the saddle to continue, but he concluded the action and retired to his monastery where he died on the 10th of December, 1041.

We know of only one coin type that can be attributed with certainty to the reign of Michael IV. It is the gold histamenon illustrated here. Fortunately for the collector, this type is not excessively rare. The bronze coins issued by Michael IV were all anonymous types.

BIBLIOGRAPHY

Fagerlie, Joan M. "A miliaresion of Romanus III and a nomisma of Michael IV", *Museum Notes* 11, 1964, pp. 227-236, (ANS, New York).

Hendy, M.F. "Michael IV and Harold Hardrada", *Numismatic Chronicle*, 1970, pp. 187-197.

Psellus, Michael. *Fourteen Byzantine Rulers, The Chronographia of Michael Psellus*, English tr. by E.R.A. Sewter, Penguin Books, New York, 1966, pp. 87-118. (Book IV on Michael IV.)

ZШH AVΓOVCTH

After Michael's death, Zoe briefly ruled alone until the adopted successor (Michael V) was crowned. Whether any coins in her name were struck during this three day period is not known—none survive. However, a few bronze patterns exist. This would seem to indicate that there was at least some contingency or intent to issue coins in Zoe's name. The elaborate crown and jewelled robe of Zoe (daughter of Constantine VIII) give us a glimpse of the opulence that was enjoyed by this descendant of the Macedonian dynasty.

It was not long before the new emperor rid himself of Zoe, having her exiled to the island of Prinkipo, where so many nobles before her had met an inglorious end. The population of the city, hearing this news, rose in a great riot and stormed the palace. Michael brought Zoe back to the palace and induced her to calm the people, but they were all the more incensed. Recognizing the gravity of his situation, he fled to the Studite monastery where he sought asylum. The passion inflamed against him at this point would allow no such reprieve and Michael was mutilated in the traditional fashion of blinding.

Zoe and her sister, Theodora, were placed on the throne as co-rulers for a brief period, during which they issued only one coin type jointly.

Zoe, AD 1041 (x1.5)
bronze pattern (reverse)
for AV histamenon nomisma

MINTS
Constantinople

BIBLIOGRAPHY

Diehl, C. *Byzantine Empresses*, tr. by H. Bell and T. de Kerpely, NY, 1963.
  Byzantine Empresses, tr. by H. Bell and T. de Kerpely, NY, 1963.
Grierson, P. *Byzantine Coins*, Berkeley, 1982, pp. 190-191.
Ostrogorsky, G. *History of the Byzantine State*, Rutgers, 1957, pp. 321-326.
Psellus, Michael. *Fourteen Byzantine Rulers, The Chronographia of Michael Psellus*, English tr. by E.R.A. Sewter, Penguin Books, New York, 1966, pp. 121-151. (Books III-V.)

+mIXAHL ΔЄΠΟt

Formerly attributed as
Michael V, AD 1041-1042
now recognized as
Michael VI

MINTS
Constantinople

Michael Kalaphates cel-ebrated his coronation by exiling his uncle John the Eunuch, who had been instrumental in his rise to the throne. Then, in a most audacious move, Kalaphates banished his adoptive mother to a convent and had her hair cut off. This insult to the great Macedonian Dynasty so out-raged the population that Kalaphates was deposed and blinded after only four months on the throne. Zoe was returned to rule, sharing the throne with her sister Theodora.

The coin illustrated here was at one time attributed to Michael Kalaphates, but is now assigned to Michael VI. Another coin (Sear 1826) which was formerly attrib-uted to Michael V has now been reassigned to Michael IV. Therefore, we are left without any coins for this ruler. The reason for this, accord-ing to Grierson (*Byzantine Coins*, p. 191), is that Zoe was "technically sovereign during his reign" and therefore no coins were struck in his name. This may well be the case, but it would not be surprising to find someday that there are indeed coins which are attributable to Kalaphates. We have included the ruler here because collectors will undoubtedly run into old references that may be confusing.

BIBLIOGRAPHY

Goodacre, Hugh. *A Handbook of the Coinage of the Byzantine Empire*, London, 1964 (reprint), pp. 226-227 (erroneously lists the above type as an issue of Michael V).

Psellus, Michael. *Fourteen Byzantine Rulers, The Chronographia of Michael Psellus*, English tr. by E.R.A. Sewter, Penguin Books, New York, 1966, pp. 121-151. (Book V.)

Sear, David R. *Byzantine Coins and Their Values*, London, 1987, p. 354 (lists the above type as an issue of Michael VI).

Constantine IX, Monomachus
cѡnstantn bASILEy Rm

After Kalaphates was deposed, the sisters Zoe and Theodora reigned jointly for a short time. They were very popular, but the people desired an emperor. This ultimately led to the marriage of Constantine Monomachus to Zoe and his elevation to the throne. Unfortunately, that did little to improve the situation. The reign of Monomachus is seen by some historians as the beginning of the final decline of the empire. Little was done to maintain the army, and the treasury was burdened by imperial extravagances.

Constantine IX, AD 1042-1055
AV histamenon nomisma
Constantinople mint

MINTS
Constantinople

On the other hand, Constantine was a patron of the arts and brought many luminaries to his court including (as secretary) Constantine (Michael) Psellus who was an adviser, philosopher and educator. In his illustrious career Psellus served nine emperors, proving that he was above all a diplomat. A lyceum was opened under the direction of the Patriarch John Xiphilinus, and a university was founded in which higher education was free to all classes—the only requirement being proper preparation.

Two notable events happened during Constantine's reign. One was the supernova in the constellation Taurus (4 July 1054), the other was the schism of the Eastern and Western churches in the same year. The supernova was observed by astronomers of the day and was probably alluded to in the design of the gold histamenon nomisma depicting Constantine with prominent stars in the fields (see illustration above). It was undoubtedly interpreted by some as a celestial sign of the schism.

BIBLIOGRAPHY

O'Hara, M.D. "An introduction to the gold coinage of Constantine IX Monomachus, AD 1042-1055", *Seaby Coin and Medal Bulletin*, 1971, pp. 46-51.

Ostrogorsky, George. *History of the Byzantine State*, Rutgers, 1957, pp. 333-337.

+ ΘΕΟΔΩΡΑ ΑΥΓΟΥΣΤΑ

Theodora, AD 1055-1056
AV tetarteron

MINTS
Constantinople

Theodora had been living in exile at the convent of Petrion since the reign of Romanus III and until the uprising against Kalaphates was virtually a forgotten member of the royal family. In their aroused passion, leaders of the revolt brought her to Hagia Sophia and crowned her empress. An agreement was reached whereby the two sisters, Zoe and Theodora would rule jointly.

When it became clear that this was an untenable solution, and Zoe was married to Constantine Monomachus, the two sisters yielded their rank. When Constantine died, some 13 years later, Theodora was again elevated to the rank of empress. Zoe had died in the meantime, and the elderly Theodora reigned alone for about a year and a half. Being the childless daughter of Constantine VIII, she was the last living descendant of the Macedonian Dynasty. Where she had deferred to Zoe in most administrative decisions of their earlier joint reign, Theodora was at this juncture ready to assume the responsibilities of state. She ruled with authority and personally decided the fate of her subjects and her empire. On August 31, 1056, Theodora died of a natural illness at the age of 76. On the details of her life and administration, we have good authority in the humanist Michael Psellus, who was her servant and confidant.

BIBLIOGRAPHY

Diehl, C. *Byzantine Empresses,* tr. by H. Bell and T. de Kerpely, NY, 1963.
Goodacre, Hugh. *A Handbook of the Coinage of the Byzantine Empire,* London, 1964 (reprint), pp. 228 and 233.
Psellus, Michael. *Fourteen Byzantine Rulers, The Chronographia of Michael Psellus,* English tr. by E.R.A. Sewter, Penguin Books, New York, 1966, (Book V, pp. 143-151 and Book VI, pp. 261-271.)

+mIXAHL AΨtOCRAt′

Michael Bringas, also known as Stratioticus, was an elderly civil servant selected by palace officials to succeed Theodora. Believing that his security rested in acceptance by the bureaucracy, he indiscriminately approved all sorts of promotions within that element of the government. This of course did not set well with the military faction and Michael found himself embroiled in a bitter power struggle.

Michael VI, AD 1056-1057
AV histamenon nomisma (x1.5)
Constantinople mint

MINTS
Constantinople

To make matters worse, Stratioticus humiliated his general Isaac Comnenus before a deputation of military leaders. This was not only tactless, it was imprudent. A rebellion sprang up within the military, and Isaac was put forth as Emperor. The stage was set for a bloody civil war. Seeing that there was not any peaceful solution, and facing widespread revolt, Stratioticus abdicated. Psellus, who was his close adviser, reports that he died soon after that as a private citizen. Others claim that he spent the rest of his life in a monastery.

The coins of Michael VI are quite rare and could not have been struck in very great quantities. The histamenon nomisma illustrated here was formerly attributed to Michael V Kalaphates (see page 84).

BIBLIOGRAPHY

Psellus, Michael. *Fourteen Byzantine Rulers, The Chronographia of Michael Psellus,* English tr. by E.R.A. Sewter, Penguin Books, New York, 1966, (Book VII), pp. 275-302.
Sear, David R. *Byzantine Coins and Their Values,* London, 1987, p. 359.
Whitting, P.D. *Byzantine Coins,* London 1973, p. 197.

The Families
Ducas, Comnenus & Angelus

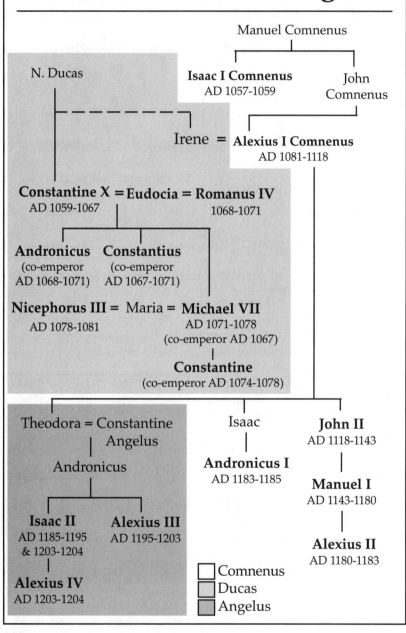

Manuel Comnenus

N. Ducas

Isaac I Comnenus
AD 1057-1059

John
Comnenus

Irene = **Alexius I Comnenus**
AD 1081-1118

Constantine X = Eudocia = **Romanus IV**
AD 1059-1067   1068-1071

Andronicus   **Constantius**
(co-emperor   (co-emperor
AD 1068-1071)   AD 1067-1071)

Nicephorus III = Maria = **Michael VII**
AD 1078-1081   AD 1071-1078
                          (co-emperor AD 1067)

Constantine
(co-emperor AD 1074-1078)

Theodora = Constantine
              Angelus

Andronicus

Isaac II   **Alexius III**
AD 1185-1195   AD 1195-1203
& 1203-1204

Alexius IV
AD 1203-1204

Isaac

Andronicus I
AD 1183-1185

John II
AD 1118-1143

Manuel I
AD 1143-1180

Alexius II
AD 1180-1183

☐ Comnenus
☐ Ducas
☐ Angelus

Isaac I, Comnenus
+ICAAKIOC BACIΛϵVC

Isaac was a prominent general and accepted the call for leadership by his troops. On assuming the throne after the abdication of Stratioticus, he quickly restrained the army by paying them tributes and sending them on furlough to their homes. By sparing the city from the inevitable outrages of a victorious military, he earned the respect and support of the civil aristocracy. Early in his reign, Isaac took firm control of the empire and oversaw all state affairs personally.

His Achilles Heel was the church. In order to finance the rebuilding of the frontiers, Isaac apparently confiscated some church property. This led to a bitter confrontation between him and the Patriarch, Michael Cerularius. The Patriarch was eventually arrested on fabricated charges of heresy and died while in prison awaiting trial. The population, being incensed by this atrocity, rose in rebellion. The outcome is a bit confusing.

According to some accounts, Isaac was forced to abdicate—just as his predecessor had done. Psellus, who claims to have been at the scene, recorded that Isaac willfully gave over the reigns of government to his chosen successor Constantine Ducas. Isaac was extremely ill, suffering from a prolonged fever, and believed himself to be on his deathbed when he announced the choice. Unexpectedly, Isaac improved but the transfer of power had already taken place. He supposedly took asylum in the monastery at Studium, where he died following a lingering illness.

Isaac I, AD 1057-1059
AV tetarteron (x1.5)
Constantinople mint

MINTS
Constantinople

BIBLIOGRAPHY

Psellus, Michael. *Fourteen Byzantine Rulers, The Chronographia of Michael Psellus*, English tr. by E.R.A. Sewter, Penguin Books, New York, 1966, (Book VII), pp. 302-330.

Wroth, W. *Imperial Byzantine Coins in the British Museum*, reprint, Chicago, 1966, pp. lvii and 511-513.

+KШN BAC Λ O ΔOVKAC

Constantine X, AD 1059-1067
AV histamenon nomisma (x1.25)
Constantinople mint

AR miliaresion, Constantinople
busts of Constantine and Eudocia

MINTS
Constantinople

Constantine Ducas was a Cappadocian noble who was actively supported by the civil aristocracy in Constantinople. Although competent as an administrator, he was not a man of broad vision. Believing that war was no longer a threat, he made the drastic mistake of reducing his military forces. This unfortunately, was done at a time when the empire was about to face serious external pressure. As a result, the Seljuq Turks were able to take large parts of Asia Minor and Armenia. In the north, the Tartar Uzes and Magyars were carving out large territories from former Romaion lands.

Ducas was married to Eudocia Makrembolitssa who is depicted with him on silver and bronze coins. They had two sons, Michael VII and Constantius.

In 1067, at the age of 60, the emperor died of an illness leaving Eudocia as regent for the two young boys. He earlier had appointed his brother John Ducas as Caesar. Although John did not share the throne, he played an important part in directing the affairs of state under this and the later reign of his nephew Michael VII.

BIBLIOGRAPHY

Ostrogorsky, George. *History of the Byzantine State*, Rutgers, 1957, pp. 341-343.

Wroth, W. *Imperial Byzantine Coins in the British Museum*, reprint, Chicago, 1966, pp. lvii and 514-520.

Eudocia, Michael VII & Constantius
+MIX ЄVΛK S KШNS

Although Eudocia was named as regent for Michael and Constantius, the actual business of government was in the hands of the Caesar, John Ducas, and the chief adviser Michael Psellus.

When it became clear that an emperor was needed, Eudocia met with a difficult situation. On his deathbed, Constantine X had willed the empire to his sons Michael and Constantius with their mother to serve as regent. (There seemingly was another son [Andronicus] that was not included for some unexplainable reason.) One of the stipulations however was a sworn oath, in writing, from Eudocia promising never to remarry. A bit of "byzantine" subterfuge saved the day, as Eudocia tricked the Patriarch into declaring that the oath was invalid as it had been extracted under duress by a jealous husband. She implied to the Patriarch that she intended to take for her husband a man named Bardas, the Patriarch's brother. Once the dissolution of the oath was confirmed, she secretly married the dashing young Romanus Diogenes.

Eudocia, Michael VII & Constantius, AD 1067
AV histamenon nomisma (x1.5)
Constantinople mint

MINTS

Constantinople

In coinage, Eudocia's regency is essentially represented by a single type—that illustrated here. A unique gold tetarteron with bust of Eudocia and Michael has also been published (Sear 1858), but it can be argued that this belongs to the two month period after the accession of Michael VII during which they ruled jointly. Following this brief span, Eudocia was involuntarily entered into a nunnery.

BIBLIOGRAPHY

Goodacre, Hugh. *A Handbook of the Coinage of the Byzantine Empire,* London, 1964 (reprint), pp. 248-249.

Psellus, Michael. *Fourteen Byzantine Rulers, The Chronographia of Michael Psellus,* English tr. by E.R.A. Sewter, Penguin Books, New York, 1966, (Book VII), pp. 345-349.

Romanus IV, Diogenes
+PШMAN ЄVΔOKIA

Romanus IV and Eudocia
AD 1068-1071
AV tetarteron (x2)

AV histamenon nomisma
Obv: Michael, Constantius & Andronicus
Rev: Christ crowning Romanus & Eudocia

MINTS
Constantinople

Romanus Diogenes, from Cappadocia, was married to Eudocia and crowned emperor on New Year's Day, 1068. Associated with him were Michael, Constantius and Andronicus—who had not previously shared the throne. Andronicus was supposedly a second son of Constantine X and Eudocia, but strangely is not mentioned in Psellus and does not appear earlier on the coins. The entire group, including Eudocia is depicted on coins struck during this reign.

The Turks were making serious advances in Asia Minor when the seasoned general marched East. As it turns out, the worst defeat in the history of the empire was suffered by Romanus at Manzikert in 1071, where the emperor himself was captured by the Turks under Alp Arslan. The captive emperor struck a deal for his release, but Michael had already been crowned emperor in his place. Romanus, although freed by the Turks, was not welcomed back at Constantinople. He was subsequently blinded with a red-hot iron and sent to a monastery where he died within a short time as a result of his injuries.

BIBLIOGRAPHY

Jenkins, R. Byzantium: *The Imperial Centuries,* New York, 1966, pp. 361-374 (Chapter on Manzikert).

Taeschner, F. "The Turks and the Byzantine Empire to the end of the thirteenth century", *Cambridge Medieval History,* IV, Pt. I, (2nd ed. 1966).

+MIXAHΛ BACIΛ O Δ

It was apparently not Michael's doing that Romanus IV was deposed and blinded. This brutal and perfidious act has been ascribed to either the Caesar, John Ducas, or Psellus. However, since we are not told of any repercussions against them, we must assume that the newly crowned Michael VII and his mother Eudocia (the wife of Romanus) accepted the action without complaint. Michael was concerned very little with affairs of state and left the management of the empire in the hands of his advisors. All of the military affairs were handled by Ducas.

Michael VII, AD 1071-1078
AV histamenon nomisma (x1.25)

Michael married a beautiful princess from Anatolia by the name of Maria, who is described in the most radiant of terms. She appears with him on a silver miliaresion.

The military faction finally revolted against Michael in 1078 and an elderly general by the name of Nicephorus Botaniates was proclaimed emperor. Michael abdicated and was named Bishop of

Michael VII & Maria
AR miliaresion (x1.5)

MINTS
Constantinople

Ephesus. Maria entered a convent at Petrion. At this point the Chronologia of Michael Psellus ends abruptly and nothing is known of his fate.

BIBLIOGRAPHY

Goodacre, Hugh. *A Handbook of the Coinage of the Byzantine Empire,* London, 1964 (reprint), pp. 256-258.

Psellus, Michael. *Fourteen Byzantine Rulers, The Chronographia of Michael Psellus,* English tr. by E.R.A. Sewter, Penguin Books, New York, 1966, (Book VII), pp. 367-380.

+ΝΙΚΗΦ ΔЄC ΤШ BOTANIAT

Nicephorus III, AD 1078-1081
EL histamenon nomisma (x1.25)
Constantinople mint

MINTS
Constantinople

The reign of Nicephorus Botaniates provided little for historians to record. He was an elderly strategus of a theme in Asia Minor and came to power in a military coup. Likewise, there were several rebellions and attempts to overthrow him in the short time that he ruled. All of these were put down by the general Alexius Comnenus.

At the time of his elevation, Nicephorus was married to a woman by the name of Berdena. She died shortly after he was crowned, and the emperor arranged to have the wife of Michael brought back to the capital. She had been living in a convent since Michael's abdication. In spite of the fact that she was still married to Michael, Nicephorus made her his consort and she once again took up residence as the empress. In fact, her effigy appears with that of Nicephorus on a silver miliaresion issued at this time. In spite of the serious financial straits of the empire, the palace was active with luxurious affairs and the people seethed with resentment.

When Alexius finally joined the ranks of the rebellious and marched on Constantinople, there was little support left for the emperor. Like his predecessors, Nicephorus took asylum in a monastery. Maria resumed her domicile in the nunnery.

BIBLIOGRAPHY

Bartusis, Mark C. "A Seal of Nikephoros Votaneiates", *ANSMN* 29, 1984, pp. 135-141.

Goodacre, Hugh. *A Handbook of the Coinage of the Byzantine Empire*, London, 1964 (reprint), pp. 259-261.

Wroth, W. *Imperial Byzantine Coins in the British Museum*, reprint, Chicago, 1966, pp. lix-lx and 535-538.

C N B B

Nicephorus Basilacius was a general of Michael VII, sent to the field against Nicephorus Bryennius who had become a threat to the imperial throne. Basilacius and Bryennius met at Thessalonica, but instead of settling the

Nicephorus Basilacius, AD 1078
AE follis, Thessalonica mint

matter in battle, they concluded a pact which gave Thessalonica to Basilacius while Bryennius marched against Constantinople. When Bryennius was defeated the citizens of Thessalonica turned over Basilacius to Alexius I. The coins of Basilacius (attributed to Bryennius in the D.O. catalogue) are exceedingly rare with only a handful of specimens surviving. The issuer's name, unfortunately, is abbreviated and we know with certainty only that it starts with the letters N and B.

The coins of Basilacius are interesting not only because of their rarity and historical importance, but because they are certainly products of a provincial mint at Thessalonica. The attribution of coins to a specific mint is very difficult during this period, and in many cases the designation of a provincial mint is speculative or conjectural. Often, the assignments are made on style, rather than epigraphical evidence. Therefore it is valuable for us to have an issue that we can say with some certainty, due to historical evidence, is from a particular provincial mint.

MINTS
Thessalonica

BIBLIOGRAPHY

Bland, Roger. "A Follis of Nicephorus Basilacius?", *Numismatic Chronicle*, 1992, pp. 175-177.
Grierson, P. "Nicephorus Bryennius or Nicephorus Basilacius?", *Numismatic Circular*, 34:1, 1976, pp. 2-3.
Sear, David R. *Byzantine Coins and Their Values*, London, 1987, p. 374.

ΝΙΚΗΦΟ ΡѠ ΔЄСΠΟ ΤΗ ΤѠ ΜЄΛΙϹΗΝѠ

**Nicephorus Melissenus,
AD 1080-1081, Lead Seal**

MINTS
Nicaea?

Nicephorus Melissenus was married to Eudocia Comnenus, the sister of the emperor Alexius I. In 1080, he was proclaimed emperor at Nicaea during a rebellion of the troops. Only a few months later, he renounced the title and joined forces with Alexius against Nicephorus Botaniates. In exchange for his loyalty he was recognized as Caesar and served Alexius faithfully until his death in 1104.

The only issue known from Melissenus is represented by a unique 2/3 miliaresion in the Bibliothèque Nationale, Paris. It measures 17mm, with the Virgin "orans" on the obverse and an inscription + [ΘΚЄ ΡΘ] ΝΙΚ[Η]ΦΟ ΡѠ ΔЄСΠΟ ΤΗ ΤѠ ΜЄ ΛΙϹΗΝѠ in five lines on the reverse (Sear 1891). It was first published in an article by Waddington in *Revue Numismatique*, 1863.

The lead seal illustrated here is similar in that the obverse also portrays the Virgin—not orans but holding Christ. The reverse inscription is nearly the same as that on the one known coin of this usurper.

BIBLIOGRAPHY

Ostrogorsky, George. *History of the Byzantine State,* Rutgers, 1957, pp. 349-350.
Sear, David R. *Byzantine Coins and Their Values,* London, 1987, p. 374.
Wroth, W. *Imperial Byzantine Coins in the British Museum,* reprint, Chicago, 1966, pp. lvii and 514-520.

+ΑΛЄIIШ ΔЄCΠOT TШ KOM

When Alexius Comnenus came to power the empire was near collapse. As his troops entered the capital there was much looting and destruction with despair raging through the capital. However, the next 37 years proved to be the salvation of Constantinople—at least temporarily. Alexius consolidated his resources, like a good commander, and prepared to address his problems one by one. With the help of creative diplomacy he was able to find help from his neighbors and gradually secure the capital against further attacks. He reorganized his army, and stabilized the economy with the introduction of a new monetary system.

Ironically, in saving the day Alexius helped seal the doom of the empire. Trade concessions given to his new allies in Venice dealt a devastating blow to the economy of Constantinople and stripped the empire of its real wealth.

Alexius I, AD 1081-1118
EL histamenon nomisma (x1.5)
Constantinople mint

MINTS
Constantinople
Thessalonica
Philippopolis?

Alexius married Irene, a granddaughter of the Caesar John Ducas, uniting these two noble families. Their son John II was named co-emperor in 1092. Their daughter Anna Comnena became one of the most famous historians of all time. Alexius died at the age of 70.

BIBLIOGRAPHY

Comnena, Anna. *The Alexiad,* English tr. by E.R.A. Sewter, Penguin, NY, 1969. (Covers AD 1069-1118.)

Grierson, P. *Byzantine Coins,* Berkeley, 1982, pp. 223-228. (Discussion of the pre-reform and post-reform coinage of Alexius I.)

Morrisson, C. " Le nomisma hyperpère avant la réforme d'Alexis Ier Comnène", *Bulletin de la Société Française de Numismatique,* 28, 1973, pp. 385-387.

John II, AD 1118-1143
Billon trachy (x1.25)
Constantinople mint

MINTS
Constantinople
Thessalonica

John Comnenus did not come to the throne through difficult circumstances. His father had lived a long and productive life and did much good for the empire. There were no uprisings to displace him on his deathbed. John himself had been co-emperor for 26 years, so he was not wanting for experience—even if he did not share the prime role with his father.

Like his father, John too married an Irene. She was the daughter of the Hungarian king, and a person of compassionate heart. She spent her days helping with charities. The two were well liked and admired by their subjects. Irene predeceased John, but he did not remarry. They had four sons. Two died before their father—Isaac and Manuel survived him.

On the military front, John continued to recapture lands in Asia Minor that had been lost in earlier reigns. In the Balkans, he completely routed the Patzinaks, ending that threat. He then went about establishing solid lines of defense to the north.

John Comnenus had been on the throne as co-emperor of senior emperor for 51 years when he met with an unfortunate accident. While hunting in Asia Minor, he injured his arm with one of his own arrows. It was either poisoned or the wound became infected and John died within a very short time. Manuel was with him at the time and, although younger than Isaac, was named successor by his father.

BIBLIOGRAPHY

Grierson, P. *Byzantine Coins*, Berkeley, 1982, pp. 229-231.
Kinnamos, John. tr. by Charles M. Brand. *Deeds of John and Manuel Comnenus*, Columbia University, 1976.

Manuel I, Comnenus
MANȢHΛ ΔЄCΠOTH

After Manuel had been given the throne by his father, word was sent to the court explaining what had happened. Isaac was quietly removed to a monastery and preparations were made to receive Manuel as emperor.

He was a flamboyant person with a flair for adventure and a penchant for Western ways. During his reign the empire was constantly at war, which he apparently took as a form of sport. He first married Irene, the daughter of Conrad III, king of Germany. When she died, in about 1158, he arranged to marry Melisend, the sister of Raymond, Count of Tripoli. Manuel left her at the altar and instead married Maria, daughter of the Prince of Antioch. He was 38, she was in her early teens. Maria gave Manuel a son, Alexius II, in about 1168.

Manuel's wars were mainly successful until 1176 when he advanced against the Seljuqs of Rum (Rome) at Iconium. Caught in an unguarded moment, his army was ambushed at Myriocephalon and nearly annihilated by the Turks. He survived, but remained in poor health and broken spirit at Constantinople for the rest of his life. Alexius II inherited the throne under the regency of Maria, but a Western regent did not set well in Constantinople and eventually she and her son were deposed and executed. No coins were struck in his name.

Manuel I, AD 1143-1180
AV hyperpyron (x1.5)
Thessalonica mint

MINTS

Constantinople
Thessalonica

BIBLIOGRAPHY

Danstrup, J. "Manuel I's coup against Genoa and Venice in the light of Byzantine commercial policy", *Classica et Mediaevalia, Revue Danoise de Philologie et d'Histoire,* 1949, pp. 195-219.

Foss, C. "A Light Electrum Trachy of Manuel Comnenus", *Numismatic Circular,* 92:1, 1984, p. 8.

Grierson, P. *Byzantine Coins,* Berkeley, 1982, pp. 231-233.

Metcalf, D.M. "The Brauron Hoard and the Petty Currency of Central Greece, 1143-1204", *Numismatic Chronicle,* 1964, pp. 251-259.

Andronicus I, Comnenus
ΑΝΔΡΟΝΙΚΟC ΔΕCΠΟΤΗC

Andronicus I, AD 1183-1185
AE tetarteron (x2)
Thessalonica mint

MINTS

Constantinople
Thessalonica

Andronicus Comnenus was a cousin of Manuel I. His rise to power came as a reaction to the regency of Maria, which was seen as influenced by the West. It was not, however at the head of an advancing army. Andronicus, apparently through intrigue, gained control of the young Alexius II (heir to Manuel) and was appointed minister. He then induced Alexius to sign the death warrant for his own mother. Andronicus was elevated to the throne as co-emperor, and he then had Alexius murdered.

The story gets more bizarre. Before Manuel's death, he had arranged the marriage of his son Alexius to Anna of France. The boy was 13, she was eight years old. After Andronicus had killed Alexius and taken the throne himself, he took Anna, the widow of Alexius, as his wife. By this time, he was 70 and she was 12.

In spite of his seamy character, Andronicus apparently was a successful diplomat and negotiator. His ultimate undoing was a crusade against the landed class in which he confiscated much property and broke the power of many feudal lords. In the process, he sent orders for the arrest of one Isaac Angelus. Not to go down without a fight, Angelus killed the emissary—which sparked a revolt of the people against Andronicus. He was caught in the streets and murdered by the crowd.

BIBLIOGRAPHY

Goodacre, Hugh. *A Handbook of the Coinage of the Byzantine Empire,* London, 1964 (reprint), pp. 282-286.
Grierson, P. *Byzantine Coins,* Berkeley, 1982, pp. 233-234.
Ostrogorsky, George. *History of the Byzantine State,* Rutgers, 1957, pp. 394-400.

Isaac, Comnenus (Cyprus)
ICCAKIOC ΔЄC

Isaac was the grandson of John II Comnenus and a great-nephew of Manuel I. Under Manuel, he was appointed as Strategus of Cilicia. During a campaign against the Armenians, he was captured and imprisoned. Finally, during the reign of Andronicus I, Isaac was ransomed from the Armenians by the Knights Templar. They were, of course, compensated for their investment by Andronicus. This was achieved mainly through the intercession of Isaac's relatives. Andronicus equipped Isaac with an army and sent him back to Tarsus.

On the way, Isaac determined to change plans and went instead to Cyprus. There, he misrepresented himself as the new governor, and when in control he declared himself emperor. This act led to severe reprisals against his family in Constantinople who had secured his freedom. When Isaac II Angelus (a second cousin of Isaac Comnenus) assumed the throne in Constantinople, he raised a fleet to retake the island. It was a poorly conceived plan, and through natural disaster and poor leadership the imperial forces were defeated. From that time on, Cyprus was ignored by Constantinople.

Issac Comnenus, AD 1184-1191
AE tetarteron, Cyprus

MINTS

Nicosia?
uncertain mints

Isaac ruled Cyprus as a tyrant for seven years, and was despised by the people of the island—especially by the rich, and leaders of the church. Avenging a personal insult, Richard Coeur-de-Lion invaded Cyprus in 1191 and met little resistance. Isaac was captured and imprisoned once more. He was finally released some years later by Amaury de Lusiguan in the hope that he would preoccupy the new emperor in Constantinople. Isaac tried in vain to win support for an overthrow, but died disconsolate and powerless.

BIBLIOGRAPHY

Bendall, Simon. "Isaac Comnenus: just a little empire on Cyprus", *The Celator*, 03:02, February 1989, pp. 1ff. (Excellent coverage, which includes a catalogue of the 13 known types struck by Isaac.)

ICAAKIOC ΔЄC

*Isaac II, AD 1185-1195
and 1203-1204
El trachy (x1.25), 1st reign
Constantinople mint*

MINTS
Constantinople
Thessalonica

Isaac Angelus, a great-grandson of Alexius I, came to power during the rebellion against Andronicus I. He spent most of his first reign unsuccessfully trying to repress the Bulgarian uprisings. He also failed in his attempt to recover Cyprus from Isaac Comnenus and it was subsequently lost to the Crusaders. The economy was also in serious trouble. The electrum trachy was severely debased during this period—consequently, the coins exhibit a very pale yellow due to the low percentage of gold. Being ineffectual in these and other affairs, Isaac was deposed and blinded by his older brother Alexius III.

Alexius fled during the Latin sack of Constantinople in 1203, and the victorious Crusaders recalled the blind Isaac to the throne after an eight year absence. He associated his son Alexius IV Angelus with him as co-emperor during this second reign. It lasted for only a short time, as the people rose in rebellion against the Latin puppet leaders and they were both killed.

Coinage for the joint reign of Isaac II and Alexius IV is rare, but specimens have been identified (see bibliography).

BIBLIOGRAPHY

Bendall, Simon. "Coinage for the Joint Reign of Isaac II, Restored, and Alexius IV (18 July 1203 - 5 Feb 1204 A.D.)", *Numismatic Circular* 87:9, 1979, pp. 382-383.

Connell, Christopher T. "The Bearded Virgin of Isaac II", *The Celator*, 10:04, April, 1996, pp. 36-38.

Sear, David R. *Byzantine Coins and Their Values*, London, 1987, p. 409.

Theodore, Mankaphas (Philadelphia)

+ΘΔPB...

Like Isaac Comnenus in Cyprus, the governor of Lydia also refused to acknowledge the authority of Isaac II, Angelus. Theodore Mankaphas first usurped the imperial title at Philadelphia in AD 1188, and struck coins, from that city or some nearby mint, in his own name. As the political situation in Constantinople began to stabilize, Theodore was forced to acknowledge Isaac Angelus as emperor. But, when the city of Constantinople fell to the Latins in 1204, Theodore again asserted his claim. He was finally deposed in 1205 by Theodore Lascaris of Nicaea.

This scyphate coin of Theodore Mankaphas was very rare until the fortuitous discovery in the early 1990s of some 60 to 70 pieces in a Eu-

Theodore Mankaphas
AD 1188-1189 and 1204-1205
Billon trachy (x1.5)

MINTS

Philadelphia?

ropean dealer's trays. It is a perfect example of the kind of discoveries which can be made in this series due to the nature of the coins themselves. To call them unimposing is to be generous. However, they are enigmatic and important. Often, it takes several specimens of a particular issue just to create a composite of the legends and iconography. Thus, the coins of this period offer the collector a wonderful opportunity to study, analyze and expose details which have never been noticed or recorded.

BIBLIOGRAPHY

Grierson, P. *Byzantine Coins*, Berkeley, 1982, pp. 235-236.
Ostrogorsky, George. *History of the Byzantine State*, Rutgers, 1957, p. 426. (Only a brief historical mention).
Wroth, W. *Imperial Byzantine Coins in the British Museum*, reprint, Chicago, 1966, pp. lxvi. (Only a brief mention which provides a reference in Nicetas Choniates to coins struck by Theodore Mankaphas. Wroth knew of no coins in this usurper's name.)

ΑΛΕΞΙΟC ΔΕCΠ

Alexius III, AD 1195-1203
EL aspron trachy (x1.5)

MINTS
Constantinople
Thessalonica

An anecdote of the coronation of Alexius III relates that upon leaving Hagia Sophia his horse reared unexpectedly and the emperor's crown was thrown from his head and broken. This poor omen pretty much says it all for the hapless emperor.

He was neither an administrator nor a leader, and we are told that much of the official business of state was conducted by his wife Euphrosyne Ducana. She attempted to initiate reforms, but this only led to increased resentment from the disenfranchised.

The frontiers were overrun and there was little left in the way of resources to secure the safety of the empire. As if this were not a large enough problem, the Fourth Crusade was assembling in Venice. In the spring of 1203, Alexius came to the realization that the Crusaders were not intent on taking the Holy Land, but rather on capturing Constantinople and reinstalling Isaac II and his son. By summer, the city was under seige. Alexius fled and on July 18, 1203 Isaac II Angelus was invited by the people to reclaim his throne, with his son Alexius IV as co-emperor. This stratagem temporarily precluded the Latin sack of the city. For more on that, see the following sections on The Latin Kingdom (p. 132).

BIBLIOGRAPHY

Grierson, P. *Byzantine Coins*, Berkeley, 1982, pp. 236-237.

O'Hara, M.D. "A hoard of electrum trachea of Alexius III", *Numismatic Chronicle*, 1977, pp. 186-188.

Metcalf, D.M. "The Istanbul Hoard of 1946 and the Date of the Neatly-Clipped Trachea, *Numismatic Circular*, 83:9, 1975, pp. 330-331.

Theodore I, Comnenus-Lascaris (Nicaea)
ΘΕΟΔΟΡΟC ΔΕCΠΟΤΗC ΚΟΜΝΗΝΟC Ο ΛΑCΚΑΡΗC

After the sack of Constantinople by the Latins, and the accompanying massacre, what was left of the nobility fled in exile to Western Greece and Asia Minor. One of the main centers of the empire in exile was at Nicaea.

Lascaris was the family name of the two Theodores from Nicaea. The adoption of the name Comnenus came only by virtue of the fact that Theodore I married a daughter of Alexius III. This, of course, was a weakly veiled grasp at legitimacy. But, it hardly mattered under the circumstances. In 1208, Theodore was crowned by the new Patriarch as the legitimate successor to the empire.

Theodore not only had the Latins to contend with, but also the Seljuqs. With their capital at Iconium, not too far south of

Theodore I, AD 1208-1222
Billon trachy, Nicaea mint
Theodore (left) and St. Theodore

MINTS
Nicaea
Magnesia

Nicaea, the Seljuqs were anxious to eliminate what they saw as an incursion. In a desperate battle, Theodore prevailed and the Sultan was killed. This led to internal power struggles within the tribe and the Seljuqs were unable to pose any immediate threat to Nicaea. Theodore methodically consolidated his resources and when he died in 1222 his successor inherited a small, but stable, empire.

BIBLIOGRAPHY

Bellinger, A. "Three more hoards of Byzantine copper coins", *ANSMN* 11, 1964, pp. 211-226.

___. "A Hoard of Silver Coins of the Empire of Nicaea", *Centennial volume of the American Numismatic Society*, 1958, pp. 73-81.

Metcalf, D.M. and M.D. O'Hara. "A Hoard of Trachea from the Reign of Theodore I of Nicaea", *Numismatic Circular*, 85:3, 1977, pp. 103-6.

Wroth, W. *Western and Provincial Byzantine Coins in the British Museum*. Argonaut reprint, Chicago, 1966, pp. lxxi and 205-209.

John III, Ducas-Vatatzes (Nicaea)
IⲰ ΔЄϹΠΟΤΙϹ Ο ΔΰΚΑϹ

Although Theodore Lascaris had a son, his fate is lost to history. John Ducas-Vatatzes was Theodore's son-in-law and it was he that came to the throne on Theodore's death. He took the solid foundation left to him and expanded it into a formidable and respected empire. At the same time that Nicaea was developing as a new imperial center, Thessalonica had been doing the same. In 1246, John captured Thessalonica and added it to his dominions—thereby consolidating Greek resistance to

John III, AD 1222-1254
AE trachy, Nicaea mint

MINTS

Magnesia
Thessalonica

the Latins. Finally, the Greeks in Epirus submitted to Nicaea in 1254.

Asia Minor was cleared of Latin contingents, and the empire in exile began to place a stranglehold on the city of Constantinople. More importantly, for the moment, was the reestablishment of the Greek cultural identity. The system of government was reestablished with attention to justice and equity. Agriculture was subsidized and churches were constructed. In short, the infrastructure of a civilization was rebuilt. To the joy of modern day numismatists, this cultural rebirth was accompanied by an extensive series of coinage in all metals.

John and Irene Lascaris, his wife of nineteen years, bore a son named Theodore who rose to the throne on his father's death. Irene had predeceased John, who subsequently married Constance, the young daughter of Frederick II of Sicily (issuer of the famed "Augustales" gold coins which imitated the Roman aureus of Augustus).

BIBLIOGRAPHY

Bendall, Simon. "John III Vatatzes and Theodore II Ducas-Lascaris" *Numismatic Circular*, 86:6, 1978, pp. 306-307.
Ostrogorsky, G. *History of the Byzantine State*, Rutgers, 1957, pp. 434-444.
Protonotarios, P. "Transitional Types of Hyperpera of John III Vatatzes' First and Second Gold Coinages", *Numismatic Circular*, 82:10, 1974, pp. 390-391.
Sear, David R. *Byzantine Coins and Their Values*, London, 1987, pp. 418-424 (An excellent catalogue of the types issued.)

Theodore II, Ducas-Lascaris (Nicaea)
ΘΕΟΔΟΡΟC ΔΕCΠΟΤΗC ΔȢΚΑC Ο ΛΑCΚΑΡΙC

Theodore was the only child of John and Irene and the continuation of the dynasty was in his hands. He was married at the age of 12 (during his father's reign) to Helen, the daughter of the Bulgarian king John Asen II. They later had a son by the name of John Lascaris.

Theodore II, AD 1254-1258
AE tetarteron, Magnesia mint

Theodore was highly educated and a prolific writer. He promoted all sorts of cultural activities within the empire. Nicaea became a humanist center which attracted learned philosophers from far afield. On the military front, he did

MINTS
Magnesia
Thessalonica

not advance the empire's boundaries, but did manage to hold off numerous advances by his enemies. It was at the court of Theodore that the first Mongol emissaries to Nicaea were received. Although he often came at odds with the nobility, Theodore was well liked by the people. Unfortunately, an advanced form of epilepsy took the life of this promising ruler while still a young man.

John Lascaris was still a minor when Theodore died and the regency was awarded to his father's friend and chief advisor, George Muzalon. This infuriated the nobility, who supported Michael Palaeologus. In a brazen attack while attending church, Muzalon was murdered—literally at the altar—and Michael gained control of the throne. Within only a few months, he was elevated to the rank of co-emperor. It has been said that at his coronation Michael and his empress left the church wearing crowns, while the young co-emperor walked behind them bareheaded.

BIBLIOGRAPHY

Ostrogorsky, G. *History of the Byzantine State*, Rutgers, 1957, pp. 444-446.
Pappadopoulos, J.B. *Théodore II Lascaris*, Paris, 1908.
Wroth, W. *Western and Provincial Byzantine Coins in the British Museum*. Argonaut reprint of 1911 edition, Chicago, 1966, pp. lxxii-lxxiii and 220-223.

Theodore, AD 1224-1230
Billon trachy (x1.25)
Thessalonica mint

MINTS
Thessalonica

Theodore Comnenus-Ducas was the half-brother of Michael Angelus, who had established the Despotate of Epirus (see page 128). He apparently used the family name Angelus in addition to that of Comnenus-Ducas. Theodore ruled at Arta after his brother's death in 1215. During this time he was responsible for the daring capture of Peter of Courtenay, the Latin Emperor of Constantinople who was enroute from his coronation in Rome to his new throne. Peter was imprisoned and died in Epirus.

In 1224, Theodore captured Thessalonica from the Latins, following a long siege. He then claimed the title *Basileus* in preference to his previous title of *Despot*. His expansion and victories continued until he ran up against the Bulgarian king John Asen II, who also had designs on taking the city of Constantinople from the Latins. Theodore was decisively defeated at Klokotnica in 1230, where he was captured and blinded.

In 1237, Theodore was released as it became apparent to the Bulgarian Czar that Nicaea was the real threat to his expansion. Hoping that Theodore could become a drain on the Nicaean resources, he was returned to Thessalonica where he installed his son John as emperor.

BIBLIOGRAPHY

Ostrogorsky, G. *History of the Byzantine State,* Rutgers, 1957, pp. 434-436.
Sear, David R. *Byzantine Coins and Their Values,* London, 1987, pp. 428-430.
Wroth, W. *Western and Provincial Byzantine Coins in the British Museum.* Argonaut reprint of 1911 edition, Chicago, 1966, pp. lxix-lxx and 193-196 (outdated, but informative—especially for early views and 19th century research).

Manuel claimed what was left of the empire of Thessalonica following the capture of his brother Theodore. Taking stock of the lands within his control, Manuel was left only with Thessalonica, Thessaly and Epirus—far less than his ambitious brother had reigned over before the Bulgarian debacle. The hopes of the Empire of Thessalonica for a restoration of the empire in Constantinople were smashed by John Asen II.

Asen then turned his attention toward the Latins in Constantinople, and surprisingly formed an alliance among the "Orthodox" rulers which included himself, Manuel of Thessalonica and John Vatatzes of Nicaea. This alliance has been seen by some historians as an opportunity for the Greeks in Nicaea and Thessalonica to establish a dialogue which eventually led to their union in 1246.

Manuel, AD 1230-1237
Billon trachy, Thessalonica mint

MINTS
Thessalonica

The known coins of Manuel Comnenus-Ducas consist only of the billon or copper trachea. They form a diverse lot, with obverse depictions of Christ, the Virgin, St. Demetrius, St. Michael and St. Theodore. The reverse typically depicts the emperor standing with or being crowned by one of these figures. The coins are of crude fabric and it is often the case that inscriptions cannot be read. Often, only a single letter or two can be discerned. They are more often identified by type than by the actual reading of the emperor's name. Specimens with readable legends or strong struck obverses should be considered a prize for collectors.

BIBLIOGRAPHY

Grierson, P. *Byzantine Coins*, Berkeley, 1982, p. 262.
Sear, David R. *Byzantine Coins and Their Values*, London, 1987, pp. 431-432.
Vasiliev, A.A. *History of the Byzantine Empire, 324-1453*, Univ. of Wisconsin, 1952, pp. 525-526.

John, Comnenus-Ducas (Thessalonica)
IШANNIC ΔЄCПOTIC

John Comnenus-Ducas,
AD 1237-1244, Billon trachy (x1.5)
Thessalonica mint

MINTS
Thessalonica

After Theodore's release from Bulgarian captivity in 1237, the blinded emperor returned to Thessalonica and reclaimed his position. Rather than occupying the throne himself, however, he installed his son John Comnenus-Ducas as emperor.

John was forced by the Nicaean emperor John Vatatzes to relinquish the title of emperor in 1243 and accept the subservient title despot. He died in 1244 and his brother Demetrius became the last ruler of Thessalonica. When Vatatzes entered Thessalonica and assumed control in 1246 he compensated Theodore with an estate near Vodena and took Demetrius in captivity back to Asia Minor.

The "Johns" and "Theodores" of Nicaea and Thessalonica are a confusing lot because of their names and the interrelationships. The coinage is all the more confusing because the names—if there are any names at all—are not clear. It is typically the case that the coins of this period are attributed by style and fabric with the assistance of data obtained from some significant and provenanced hoards. There are many reattributions in this series and it is well to be cautious of older references. The most current information often comes from articles published in scholarly numismatic journals.

BIBLIOGRAPHY

Bendall, Simon. "Thessalonican coinage of the mid-thirteenth century in the light of a new hoard", *Numismatic Chronicle,* 1978, pp. 105-115.
Bertelè, T. "Monete do Giovanni Comneno Duca imperatore di Salonicco (1237-44)", *Numismatica,* xvi, 1950, pp. 61-79.
Ostrogorsky, G. *History of the Byzantine State,* Rutgers, 1957, pp. 439-440.

The Palaeologan Dynasty

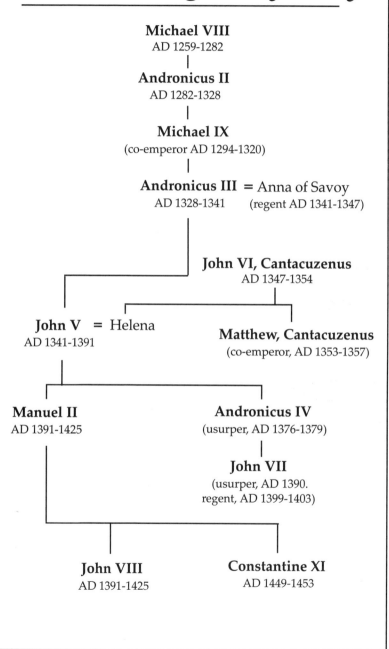

Michael VIII
AD 1259-1282

Andronicus II
AD 1282-1328

Michael IX
(co-emperor AD 1294-1320)

Andronicus III = Anna of Savoy
AD 1328-1341   (regent AD 1341-1347)

John VI, Cantacuzenus
AD 1347-1354

John V = Helena
AD 1341-1391

Matthew, Cantacuzenus
(co-emperor, AD 1353-1357)

Manuel II
AD 1391-1425

Andronicus IV
(usurper, AD 1376-1379)

John VII
(usurper, AD 1390.
regent, AD 1399-1403)

John VIII
AD 1391-1425

Constantine XI
AD 1449-1453

X̄M ΔЄϹΠΟΤ Ο ΠΑΛЄΟΛΟΓ

Michael VIII, AD 1261-1282
AV hyperpyron (x1.5)
Constantinople mint

MINTS

Magnesia
Thessalonica
Constantinople

As the co-emperor of Nicaea from 1258-1261, Michael concentrated his efforts toward recapturing the city of Constantinople. On the 15th of August, 1261, that ambition was realized when one of Michael's generals took the city. As Michael prepared to make his entrance, there was still the issue of the young son of Theodore. Michael Palaeologus, founder of one of the empire's greatest dynasties, had the innocent child blinded and deposed—an act which remained a blemish on the great family name for nearly two centuries.

Aside from that, Michael was a master diplomat and his skills were more effective than the sword against covetous Western princes. Through a series of alliances and trade agreements, he was able to shield the empire against invasion and secure the time to rebuild Constantinople as a dominant force in the region. He issued an extensive series of coinage from three mints. When Michael died in 1282 the restored empire passed peacefully to his son and heir Andronicus Palaeologus.

BIBLIOGRAPHY

Bendall, S. and P.J. Donald. "The Silver Coinage of Michael VIII, AD 1258-1282", Numismatic Circular, 90:4, 1982, pp. 121-124.

Bendall, S. "A New Type of 'Billon ' Trachy of Michael VIII?", Numismatic Circular, 87:12, 1979, p. 549.

Bendall, S. and P.J. Donald. The billon trachea of Michael VIII Palaeologos, 1258-1282, London, 1974.

___. "An early Palaeologan gold hoard", Numismatic Chronicle, 1982, pp. 66-82.

Geanakoplos, D.J. The Emperor Michael Palaeologus and the West, Harvard, 1959.

Andronicus II & Michael IX
ANΔPONIKOC ЄN XШ ΔЄCΠOTIC O ΠAΛ

Andronicus was raised to the rank of co-emperor with his father Michael VIII in 1272 and coins of their joint rule were issued at Constantinople and Thessalonica. He inherited the throne in 1282, and coins of his sole reign are fairly common. Although Andronicus maintained a court of refinement and promoted cultural activities, he was not the statesman that his father was. Under his reign the true weakness of the empire became apparent. Andronicus elevated his son Michael IX to the rank of co-emperor in 1295 and once again coins of the joint reign were issued.

Michael died prematurely in 1320 and his son Andronicus III

Andronicus II & Michael IX
AD 1295-1320
AR basilikon (x1.25)

MINTS
Constantinople
Thessalonica

petitioned for the share of the throne that his father had held. This was unacceptable to the senior Andronicus and the resulting controversy led to a civil war. In 1325 Andronicus III was accepted as co-emperor. Further, in 1328 Andronicus II was forced to relinquish the government to his grandson. He was stripped of authority, but apparently retained his titles because coins struck in the name of Andronicus II and Andronicus III have been dated from 1325 to 1334.

BIBLIOGRAPHY

Bendall, S. "A Coin from the Joint Reign of Andronicus II and Michael IX with the sole effigy of Andronicus II", *Num. Circular,* 92:1, 1984, pp. 5-6.
___. "A Thessalonican Hyperpyron of Andronicus II and Michael IX?", *Numismatic Circular* 89, 1981, p. 158.
___. "Andronicus II and Michael IX—an overdate", Numismatic Circular, 87:5, 1979, p. 134.
Ostrogorsky, G. *History of the Byzantine State,* Rutgers, 1957, pp. 481-498.
Protonotarios, P. "Is a reattribution of the hyperpyron of the 'Proskynesis' type justified?", *Numismatic Circular,* 82, 1974, pp. 283-285.
Whitting, Philip. "Miliaresia of Andronicus II and Michael IX", *Numismatic Circular,* 80:7-8, pp. 270-274 and 80:9, pp. 324-326 both 1972.

ANΔPONIKOC AVTOKPATOP

Andronicus III, AD 1328-1341
Billon trachy, Constantinople

MINTS
Constantinople
Thessalonica

It is hard to imagine why Andronicus III was so intent on ascending the throne. His reign was wracked by civil war, the loss of Asia Minor, the rise of the Serbs and corruption in the imperial bureaucracy. There were very few bright spots on the horizon.

To his credit, Andronicus faced the problems head on. He appointed John Cantacuzenus as chief minister and basically left the affairs of State in his hands. Andronicus led the increasingly frequent military campaigns.

Andronicus married Irene of Brunswick, who died five years later. He then married Jeanne of Savoy, whose name was changed to Anna. They had a son, John V, who inherited the throne as a minor when his father died in 1341.

The coins of Andronicus III are of very crude fabric and design. They also are quite scarce, although there are a fair number of types attributed to this ruler. One interesting hyperpyron (Grierson 1295) portrays on its obverse Andronicus and Anna standing. On the reverse is a kneeling figure of John V being crowned by Christ. It has been suggested by Grierson that this is an issue of the regency of Anna, representing the posthumous Andronicus. There are several other varieties in this reign that despite their crude execution are quite interesting from an iconographic perspective.

BIBLIOGRAPHY

Bertelè, T. *Monete e sigilli di Anna di Savoia, Imperatrice di Bisanzio,* Rome, 1937.

Gerassimov, Theodor. "Les hyperpères d'Andronic II et d'Andronci III et leur circulation en Bulgarie", *Byzantinobulgarica,* 1, 1962, pp. 213-236.

Grierson, P. *Byzantine Coins,* Berkeley, 1982, pp. 287 and 292-293.

Ostrogorsky, G. *History of the Byzantine State,* Rutgers, 1957, pp. 499-510.

Veglery, A. and A. Millas. "Gold Coins for Andronicus III", *Numismatic Circular,* 86:12, 1973, pp. 467-469 and 87:1, 1974, pp. 4-7 and 87:2, 1974, pp. 50-51.

John VI, Cantacuzenus
KTKZN ГОΔ ΔMTP

John VI, AD 1347-1354
AR basilikon

MINTS
Constantinople

John Cantacuzenus was a wealthy aristocrat, who came to power in 1341 as regent for John V Palaeologus. Actually, he had taken the capital by force but accepted the role of regent to satisfy his opposition. He was crowned co-emperor in 1347, with his wife Irene at his side as empress. Cantacuzenus was undoubtedly a patriotic and well-intentioned ruler—pouring much of his personal wealth into the state. He raised his own son, Matthew, to the rank of co-emperor in 1354.

Matthew was also designated Despot of the Morea, which Cantacuzenus established as a separate district. It was the one place left where Romaion culture flourished. There were constant power struggles within the court, and at one time Matthew was even designated as superior to John V.

In a specious show of unity, John V and Helena—the daughter of Cantacuzenus—were married. Although it seems that they became happy in the union, relations with Cantacuzenus were deteriorating. Civil war broke out, and John V was exiled to Tenedos.

In 1354, with the help of the Genoese, John V reoccupied Constantinople and Cantacuzenus abdicated. He retired to a monastery, where he spent the rest of his days as the monk Joasaph writing the history of his time. In spite of the fact that it is a biased account, his work is one of our principal sources for this information on this period.

BIBLIOGRAPHY

Bertelè, Tommaso. "Monete dell'imperatore Giovanni VI Cantacuzeno", *Mélanges Georges Ostrogorsky I*, Belgrade, 1973, pp. 43-59.

Nicol, Donald M. *The Byzantine Family of Kantakouzenos*, Dumbarton Oaks Studies XI, 1968.

Veglery, A. and A. Millas. "The Silver Coinage of John VI, Cantacuzenus (1353-1354)", *Numismatic Circular*, 80:9, 1972, pp. 310-311.

IѠ ΔЄСΠΟΤΙϹ Ο ΠΑΛЄΟΛΟΓΟϹ

John V was nine years old when he succeeded his father, Andronicus III. This led immediately to a confrontation between John Cantacuzenus, the councillor of Andronicus, and John Kalekas, the Patriarch. Anna of Savoy, the boy's mother, supported the latter.

After a six year struggle, John Cantacuzenus occupied Constantinople and an agreement was reached whereby John Palaeologus and John Cantacuzenus (now John VI) would jointly share the throne. Anna remained in Thessalonica as sole ruler of that city.

John V was 25 years old when Cantacuzenus was finally forced to abdicate. His long reign was filled with misfortune including the usurpation of power by his own son, Andronicus IV, and his grandson John VII. During this time, the empire fell to its lowest level when it ultimately became a vassal state of the Ottoman Sultan.

John V, AD 1341-1391
AR hyperpyron (x1.25)

John V and Anna of Savoy
AD 1341-1347, AR basilikon (x1.25)

MINTS

Constantinople
Thessalonica

BIBLIOGRAPHY

Bendall, S. and D. Nicol. "Anna of Savoy at Thessalonica: the numismatic evidence", *Revue Numismatique,* 1977, pp. 87-102.

Brunetti, Lodovico. "Sulla quantità di moneta d'argento emesse sotto Anna di Savoia imperatrice di Bisanzio (1341-1347)" [with comments by Tomasso Bertelè], *Rivista italiana di numismatica e scienze affini,* 65, 1963, pp. 143-168.

Gerasimov, Theodor. "Les hyperpèrs d'Anne de Savoi et di Jean V Paléologue", *Byzantinobulgarica,* 2, 1966, pp. 329-335.

Protonotarios, P.N. "John V and Anna of Savoy in Thessalonica (1351-1365): the Sevres Hoard", AJN 2, 1990, pp. 119-128.

ANΔPONIKOV ΔЄCΠOTOV

The tales of byzantine intrigue are endless, and no doubt the motivation for coining the word, but few accounts are more bizarre than the story of Andronicus IV. As John V's eldest son, Andronicus was being groomed for the role of emperor, and was married to Maria, the daughter of Alexander of Trebizond. He was not content, however, to wait for his natural succession.

Andronicus conspired with the son of the Turkish Sultan to overthrow both of their fathers (perhaps also with the help of the Genoese).

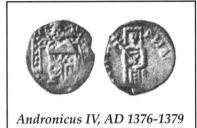

Andronicus IV, AD 1376-1379
AR basilikon? (x1.5)

MINTS
Constantinople

The attempt, however, was unsuccessful. The young Turk was blinded, and the Sultan sent Andronicus to his father in chains with orders to exact the same punishment. As a vassal of the Sultan, John could not refuse—even if he preferred a different action. However, through some quirk of fate, incompetence or intention, the young prince retained sight in one eye. Not to be denied, he gathered his forces once again and this time (1376) managed to take the city. Andronicus imprisoned his father, and was crowned emperor. He associated his son John with him as co-emperor.

During this period Andronicus issued a few silver and bronze coins, which are all scarce or rare today. In 1379, John V obtained his freedom with Turkish help and retook the capital. An agreement was reached making Andronicus the designated successor but he died in 1385. Since John V had chosen to ignore the claim of his grandson, this left Manuel II first in line for the throne.

BIBLIOGRAPHY

Goodacre, Hugh. *A Handbook of the Coinage of the Byzantine Empire,* London, 1964 (reprint), pp. 339 and 347-349.
Grierson, P. *Byzantine Coins,* Berkeley, 1982, pp. 287-288.
Vasiliev, A.A. *History of the Byzantine Empire, 324-1453,* Univ. of Wisconsin, 1952, p. 586.

Manuel II, Palaeologus
MANOVHΛ ΔЄCΠOTIC

Manuel II, AD 1391-1423
AR 1/2 stavraton
Constantinople mint

MINTS

Constantinople
Thessalonica

When the Turkish Sultan Bayazid began a determined siege of Constantinople in 1394, Manuel II appealed to the West for aid. A Crusader force responded in 1396, but was destroyed at the Battle of Nicopolis. In 1399, a small French force broke through the Turkish lines and entered the city. Seizing this opportunity, Manuel left under their escort to make a personal appeal for help. He put his nephew, John VII, in charge and went first to Venice, then to Paris and even London.

While in France, Manuel was the guest of the famous Jean Duc du Berry. He spent two years enjoying the hospitality of the French court, receiving every courtesy, but no relief for his besieged city. His journey lasted until 1402, but did not produce military aid from any of the monarchies of Europe. Fortuitously, the Turks fell under attack from the East at this time by Timur the lame (Tamerlane). Consequently, they were forced to abandon the siege of Constantinople—at least for a time. Unfortunately, the empire was so depleted at this point that it could not follow up on its good fortune and mount an attack against the Turks. By the end of Manuel's reign they had regained their strength and were once again threatening to take the capital.

The stavrati of Manuel, like those of John VII, John VIII and Constantine XI, were designed as an ultimate abstraction. The images are composed merely of lines and circles.

BIBLIOGRAPHY

Barker, J.W. *Manuel II Palaeologos, 1391-1425, a study in late Byzantine statesmanship*, Rutgers, 1969.
Barton, John L. "Byzantine Emperor links past to present", *The Celator*, 01:04, Aug/Sep 1987, pp. 1ff.
Dennis, G.T. *The Reign of Manuel II Palaeologus in Thessalonica (1382-7)*, Orientalia Christiana Analecta, Rome, 1960.

John VII, Palaeologus
ΙШΑΝΙC ΒΑCΙΛΕVC Ο ΠΑΛΕΟΛΟΓΟC

John VII was the grandson of John V that had been rejected a few years earlier due to the insurrection of his father. In spite of the fact that an agreement had been reached in 1381 assuring his position as successor, it must have been clear that neither John V nor Manuel had any intention of living up to the agreement.

In 1390, with the help of Sultan Bayazid, the young John rebelled against his grandfather, who was still on the throne. This must have been more than a little disconcerting since John V had suffered the revolt of his own son earlier and now that of his grandson. The revolt succeeded temporarily and John VII was installed as emperor for about five months.

*John VII, AD 1390
and regent 1399-1402
AR 1/4 hyperpyron (x1.25)*

MINTS
Constantinople

Manuel II, who had been in the field, came to his father's aid, however, and John V was free again. There must not have been a great deal of animosity over the issue, because John VII was later chosen as regent to run the government while Manuel was on his extended trip to European capitals seeking aid.

There are only three coin types known for John VII; a silver 1/4 hyperpyron, a copper tornese, and a copper follaro. They all present the effigy of the emperor on the obverse and saints on the reverse. All of the types are scarce or rare.

BIBLIOGRAPHY

Charanis, P. "The Strife Among the Palaeologi and the Ottoman Turks, 1370-1402", *Byzantion*, 16, 1942/3, pp. 286-315.

Dölger, F. "Johannes VII, Kaiser der Rhomäer 1390-1408", *Byzantinische Zeitschrift* 31, Leipzig, 1931, pp. 21-36.

Vasiliev, A.A. *History of the Byzantine Empire, 324-1453*, Univ. of Wisconsin, 1952, p. 586 and 631-632.

IѠΑΗC ΔЄCΠΟΤΙC Ο ΠΑΛЄΟΛΟΓΟC

John VIII, AD 1423-1448
AR stavraton
Bust of Christ / bust of John

MINTS

Constantinople

John, the eldest son of Manuel II inherited the throne in 1423 and reigned for 25 years—a remarkably long time considering the dismal state of affairs the empire found itself in. It was in reality no longer an empire, but a principality, with a sister city (Mistra) in the Peloponnesus.

All that was left at this point was to pay the tributes demanded and implore the aid of the West. The requests for assistance fell on deaf ears and the countdown to the final hours began.

John married three times—all in hope, one suspects, of receiving aid from an "in-law". The first was to a Russian princess, Anna, daughter of the Grand Prince of Moscow. She fell victim to the plague and died after three years in Constantinople. Next, John married an Italian—Sophia of Montferrat. She was poorly received and unhappy at the court. With the help of the Genoese she ran off to Italy and entered a convent. Finally, John married a beautiful princess from Trebizond by the name of Maria. She charmed the court and the people, but did not outlive her husband. John did not have any children by his three wives and left the throne vacant when he died in 1448.

The coins of John VIII, like those of his immediate predecessors, are remarkable for their stylized imagery which is abstracted to the point of being pure line (see page 23). In spite of the fact that there are only a few varieties, they are quite common.

BIBLIOGRAPHY

Bendall, Simon. "A Hoard of Silver Coins of John VIII, 1423-1428", *Numismatic Circular*, 86:1, 1978, pp. 14-15.

Connell, Christopher T. "Icon of Christ on coins of John VIII is remarkable for its abstract imagery", *The Celator*, 05:12, December 1991, pp. 36 ff.

Vasiliev, A.A. *History of the Byzantine Empire, 324-1453*, Univ. of Wisconsin, 1952, p. 588.

КШNCT...ПАΛ

Constantine XI was the eighth of ten children born to Manuel II and Irene. Strangely enough, his accession was aided by the Sultan Murad II who was technically the suzerain of the city. When Constantine came to the throne he inherited only the city of Constantinople and a small strip of land in the Peloponnesus called the Morea. The empire was at that point completely at the mercy of the Turks. In 1453 the final breath was drawn as Muhammad II stormed the walls which were severely battered by cannon fire and beyond repair.

Constantine XI, AD 1448-1453
AR stavraton, Constantinople

MINTS
Constantinople

Constantine met the final challenge personally, fighting hand to hand on the ramparts and refusing all pleas to make his escape. It is said that he was offered rule of the Morea in exchange for his surrender, but he refused. After the battle, his mutilated body was identifiable only by the imperial emblems on garments that he wore. His heroic stand earned Constantine XI a lasting place in history and a place in the folk legends of the Romaion people. It must have seemed ominous at the time that the first and last rulers of Rome were named Romulus and the first and last rulers of Constantinople were named Constantine.

The coins of Constantine XI were virtually unknown until a small hoard appeared on the market in the last decade (see page 134). They still are very rare, but specimens occasionally show up at auction. These coins were apparently struck during the final days of the empire, perhaps only days before the fall of Constantinople to the Turks.

BIBLIOGRAPHY

Bendall, Simon. "The Coinage of Constantine XI", *Société Francaise de Numismatique*, 1991.
___. "A Coin of Constantine XI", *Num. Circular*, 82:5, 1974, pp. 188-189.
Berk, Harlan J. "Artistic examination permits re-evaluation of Constantine XI's coinage", *The Celator*, 07:02, Feb. 1993, pp. 28-29.
Jones, J.R. "Literary Evidence for the Coinage of Constantine XI", *Numismatic Circular*, 75, 1967, p. 97.

Index to Emperors and Empresses

An inscription on a column in the Church of the Forty Martyrs at Trnovo, Bulgaria reads in part: "I, John Asen, in Christ God the faithful Tsar and Autocrat of the Bulgars . . . set forth on a march upon Romania and defeated the Greek troops, and I have captured the Emperor himself, Theodore Comnenus... ." John Asen was not, of course, recording his advance into the modern country of Rumania, but into the lands of the Romaion or "Byzantine" empire. To him, the Greek lands were "Romania" or the Roman empire. The fact that he refers to its inhabitants as Greeks underscores the essence of the term *Romaion,* which the Greek speaking successors of the Romans used in reference to themselves.

The extent of the empire varied greatly from one period to the next, at one time including the entire Mediterranean region and at another only the city of Constantinople and a tiny principate in southern Greece. The ebb and flow of power is complex, and tracing it goes far beyond the scope of this book As a very brief and general introduction to the more important centers of power, we have included in the following pages a series of geographical vignettes. These are arranged more or less in the fashion that Greek coins are catalogued. That is, starting at the northwest corner of the Mediterranean and proceeding east to the Levant, then south to Egypt, and finally west into North Africa. Where appropriate, we have included maps to help define the locations being discussed.

Although geography itself is seldom a defining criteria for the collector of these coins, it is conceivable that one might choose to collect a coin from each mint, or focus on a theme of imperial expansion. More likely, collectors will focus on the coins of a particular reign or a particular place. For example, the coins of Cherson, Trebizond , Antioch or Alexandria might present sufficient challenge. One notable numismatist specializes in coins of the Palaeologans. Another well known collector specializes in the coins of the seventh century. There are many collectors of the imitative coins that fall into the general class "Arab-Byzantine". It is our intention here to expose the reader to the variety of possibilities, so that one can choose a path with somewhat less wandering.

Spain

Justinian's program of imperial expansion finally took him to Spain in AD 550. At first, he sent a small fleet. Prevailing at one encounter after another, they managed to take the southeast corner of the Iberian peninsula from the Visigoths. Included in this territory were the cities of Carthagena, Malaga and Cordova. These captured cities remained under imperial control for about seventy-five years. The Visigoths eventually rebounded, under the leadership of Suinthila, and the Roman settlements were lost about 624. Heraclius did manage to retain control of the Balearic Islands. This short occupation of a rather small district is not significant in itself. But, the fact that the Eastern Romans were able even to secure a toehold this far west was a major source of pride and prestige.

The Roman coinage struck in Spain is far from abundant. Although other types may come to light, only one coin has been assigned to a Spanish mint under Justinian. It is a gold tremissis of the standard type with diademed bust obverse and Victory on the reverse (see Grierson, below). It is conjectured that the mint was at Carthagena. A similar tremissis was issued in Spain by Justin II. No coins from Spain have been noted for the reign of Tiberius II Constantine, but his successor Maurice Tiberius issued at least two varieties of the tremissis there. A single issue each is known for the reigns of Phocas and Heraclius. Both are tremisses. The attribution of these coins has been determined mainly by the discovery of coins bearing similar styles and fabric, with known provenance. Wroth does not list any issues from this province—because they were not known at that time. The tremisses from Spain are distinguished by their poor metal and distinctive style (See Grierson, *Byzantine Coins*, no. 54 and 55).

Bibliography — Spain

Bouchier, E. *Spain under the Roman Empire*, Oxford, 1914.
Grierson, P. *Byzantine Coins*, Berkeley, 1982, p. 56 and no. 54-55.
___. "Une ceca bizantina en España", *Numario hispanico*, Madrid, 1955, pp. 305-314.
Mateu y Llopis, Felipe. "La moneda bizantina en España", *Crónica del III Congesso arqueológico del sudeste español*, Murcia, 1947, Cartagena, 1948, pp. 310-320.

After the fall of Rome, Italy became a Teutonic kingdom. They issued their own coinage, which was modelled after that of their Western Roman predecessors or after coinage from the Eastern empire. The Ostrogoths ruled from 476 to 553 when they were finally crushed by the army of Justinian at the battle of Mons Lactarius. At that time, Ravenna and Rome were back in the hands of the Romans and coins were struck for Justinian at several Italian mints as well as in Sicily. The victory was short lived, as the Lombards invaded in 568. Ravenna and Rome held out while the outlying areas were absorbed, but Ravenna eventually fell in 751.

*Ostrogoths, AE follis
Theodoric, AD 522-534*

*Beneventum, AV solidus
Romoald, AD 706-731*

The Lombards ruled Italy for about two centuries and were finally displaced by Charlemagne in 774. Of the four Lombard duchies, the preeminent one was Beneventum—which produced coinage in imitation of that from Constantinople. Venice began its rise to prominence under the Carolingian kings, while Genoa developed a powerful merchant class. Eventually, Italy became a feudal battleground as principalities and their nobles competed for supremacy under various overlords.

*Ravenna, AE 40 nummi
Heraclius, dated AD 633/34*

The Romans held Sicily longer than they did Spain or Italy, and the island was an important center politically, strategically and financially. Constans II even relocated his residence to Syracuse. In the ninth century, Sicily fell under Muslim attack and the island gradually was lost to the invaders. By the end of the reign of Michael III only Syracuse and Taormina (Tauromenium) were still in the hands of the Romans. Despite a valiant attempt by Basil I to reclaim the territories in Sicily and southern Italy, the Arabs prevailed and Sicily fell in 902.

Constans II, AD 641-668
AE 40 nummi, Syracuse mint

Having ruled for twenty years from Constantinople, Constans II suddenly decided to leave the city and move his residence west—specifically to Syracuse. In 654 he elevated his son Constantine IV to co-emperor, and his two younger sons to that rank in 659. Then, during a tour of imperial holdings in 663, he set up residence in Sicily—never returning to Constantinople.

Bibliography — Sicily & Italy

Bratianu, G.I. "L'Hyperpère byzantine et la monnaie d'or des republiques italiennes", Etudes byzantines d'histoire economique et sociale, Paris, 1938, pp. 225-237.

Donald, P.J. "The Neapolis Coins of Heraclius", *Numismatic Circular*, 94:4, 1986, p. 116.

Fairhead, N. and W. Hahn. "The Monte Judica Hoard and the Sicilian Moneta Auri under Justinian I and Justin II", Hahn & Metcalf, ed., *Studies in Early Byzantine Gold Coinage*, ANSNS 17, NY, 1988, pp. 29-39.

Grierson, P. & M. Blackburn. *Medieval European Coinage*, Cambridge, 1986.

Maull, I. "Le zecche dell'antica Ravenna (402-404-751 d.C.)", *Felix Ravenna* 84, 1961, pp. 79-134.

Sambon, A. "L'atelier monétaire de Syracuse do VIe au VIIIe siècle de l'ère chrétienne", *Le Musée*, 3, 1906, pp. 267-273.

Spahr, R. *Le Monete Siciliane Dai Bizantini a Carlo D'Angelo*, Zurich, 1976.

Wroth, W. *Western and Provincial Byzantine Coins in the British Museum*. Argonaut reprint of 1911 edition, Chicago, 1966.

The Western Lands
of Romania

Thessalonica / Epirus

Michael I, Angelus was a cousin of Isaac II and Alexius III who founded the Despotate of Epirus after the fall of Constantinople to the Latins. His father had earlier been governor of the district, and he settled there after an unsuccessful attempt to displace the Franks from the Morea. A rare silver trachy is the only known coinage of his reign. He was murdered by a court servant in 1215 and was succeeded by his half-brother Theodore Comnenus-Ducas. In 1224 Theodore conquered the Latin kingdom of Thessalonica. This established a Western successor which rivalled the exiled empire in Nicaea. In a desperate battle with Bulgarian forces under John Asen II, Theodore was captured and blinded. His place was taken by his brother, Manuel Comnenus-Ducas. Manuel ruled for 7 years, but the blinded Theodore returned and Manuel was deposed in 1237.

Michael II, Angelus was a nephew of Manuel Comnenus-Ducas. Shortly before he was deposed, Manuel granted the Despotate of Epirus to Michael. He apparently issued silver and copper coins. In 1246, John Vatatzes (Nicaea) captured Thessalonica, but Michael was left in control at Arta in Epirus. Coins were then issued in their joint names.

Wroth mentions that John I Angelus, the illegitimate son of Michael II of Epirus, established a Duchy at Neopatras in 1271. He was granted the title Sebastocrator and issued coins. His successors included Constantine Angelus (1296-1303) and John II Angelus-Comnenus (1303-1318). Little is known about these dukes.

The coinage of Epirus and Thessalonica is just now being unraveled, see the Gallery of Emperors (pages 108-110) for more details.

Bibliography — Thessalonica / Epirus

Bendall, Simon. "Longuet's Salonica Hoard Reexamined", *ANSMN* 29, 1984, pp. 143-157.

___. "Palaeologan gold coins from the Mint of Thessalonica", *Schweizer Münzblatter* 125, Feb. 1982, pp. 15-21.

Grierson, P. *Byzantine Coins*, Berkeley, 1982, pp. 255-267.

Mattingly, Harold. "A find of thirteenth century coins of Arta in Epirus", *Numismatic Chronicle*, 1923, pp. 31-46.

Metcalf, D.M. *The copper coinage of Thessalonica under Justin I*, Vienna, 1976.

___. *Coinage in the Balkans, 820-1355*, Thessaloniki, 1965.

___. "The coinage of Thessaloniki, 829-1204, and its place in Balkan monetary history", *Balkan Studies*, 4, 1963, pp. 277-288.

Nicol, D.M. *The Despotate of Epirus*, Oxford, 1957.

Wroth, W. *Western and Provincial Byzantine Coins in the British Museum*. Argonaut reprint of 1911 edition, Chicago, 1966.

The Morea

Following the Latin capture of Constantinople in 1204, and the subsequent division of lands formerly under control of the empire, the Franks established in the Peloponnesus the feudal principality of Achaia—also known as the Morea with its center at Mistra. In spite of their generally weak position, the French managed to hold this region for three quarters of a century. However, the successful campaigns of Michael VIII regained much of this territory. By the time of Andronicus II, it had been completely retaken and was placed under the control of Cantacuzenus, the father of the later emperor John VI. During the latter's reign, the administration of lands was further decentralized and John transferred the dependency of Morea to his son Manuel. From this time on the ruling authority of the Morea assumed the title *despot*.

In the civil war between John V Palaeologus and John VI Cantacuzenus, the Morea fell to the Palaeologans and stayed in their hands until its eventual fall to the Turks in 1460—seven years after the empire at Constantinople had finally collapsed.

There were no Romaion coins known to be struck in the Morea. One coin is known of Matthew Cantacuzenus, in his own name, but it is presently assigned to the Constantinople mint (Sear 2543). Coinage of the neighboring Latins was the primary monetary instrument.

Despots of the Morea	
Manuel Cantacuzenus (son of John VI)	1348-1380
Matthew Cantacuzenus (son of John VI)	1380-1383
Demetrius Cantacuzenus (son of Matthew)	1383
Theodore I, Palaeologus (son of John V)	1383-1407
Theodore II, Palaeologus (son of Manuel II)	1407-1443
Constantine & Thomas (sons of Manuel II)	1443-1449
Thomas & his son Demetrius	1449-1460

Bibliography — The Morea

Loenertz, R.J. "Pour l'histoire du Péloponèse au XIVe siècle (1382-1404)", *Revue des Etudes Byzantines* I, Bucharest, 1943, pp. 152-196.
Longnon, *L'Empire latin de Constantinople et la princiaouté de Morée*, Paris, 1949.
Schmitt, J. *Die Chronik von Morea. Eine Untersuchung über das Verhältnis ihrer Handschriften und Versionen*, Munich, 1889, English translation London, 1904.
Zakythinos, D. *Le despotat grec de Morée*. I and II, Paris, 1932-53.

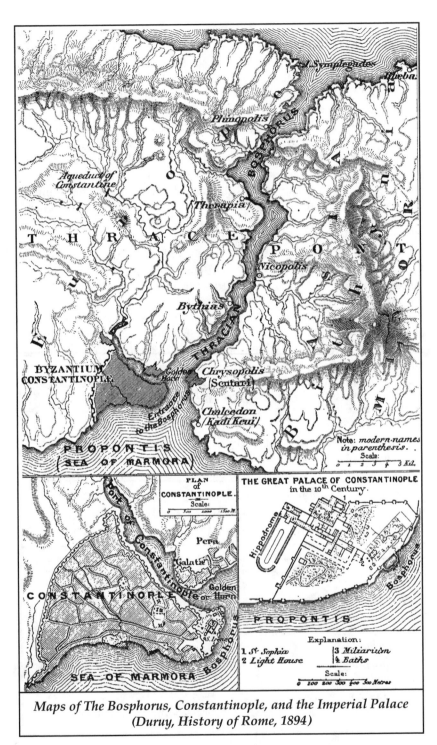

Maps of The Bosphorus, Constantinople, and the Imperial Palace
(Duruy, History of Rome, 1894)

Constantinople

Constantinople—the city on the Golden Horn! The very name inspires feelings of romance and intrigue. At the time of Justinian I, the city of Constantinople covered eight square miles and had some 500,000 inhabitants. It was a place of great splendor and untold wealth. Visitors from all of the world marvelled at its vitality and at the richness of its culture. Some of them wrote about what they saw, and their words move us to this day.

The city was perfectly located, with command of the sea routes north to south. It was also well located to respond to external threats. Easy access to the Danube and the East, both by land and sea, made it a perfect marshalling point for military campaigns. Equally important, this access made the city a perfect emporium for trade to these outlying areas. Of course it also made Constantinople a target for invaders from many lands—and for ambitious pretenders who coveted the throne of this great jewel. From as early as AD 400, citizens of Constantinople were called upon to defend their city against external forces. It never stopped, at least not for long, in the 1,000 year history of the city.

Constantinople was also the most important religious center in the East. Only Rome was its equal—and that was something you believed only if you were from the West. The great churches, like Hagia Sophia, and monasteries filled with treasures beyond description, are impressive even as skeletons. To imagine what they were like in their prime is impossible.

The numismatist recognizes Constantinople as having one of the most prolific mints in the history of coinage. The variety and complexity of types, denominations and imagery are staggering to comprehend. Even today, after centuries of research and diligent study by generations of numismatists, there are many areas that remain virtually untouched. Fortunately, we have a large body of primary sources to help us understand the city, its people, and the coins which they used in everyday commerce.

There are two great episodes in the history of the city that were particularly important from a numismatic perspective. These were the two times that the city fell. In 1204, when the Latin knights of the Fourth Crusade captured the city, and again in 1453 when Mehmet the Conqueror brought the city to its final end, emergency issues tell the story of impending disaster. Another peculiarity, which is related in a way, is the *Politikon* coinage that circulated within parts of the city as a sort of "Western" currency. On the following pages, we offer a brief discussion of the coins that fall into these three interesting categories which are more about the city of Constantinople than about the empire at large.

The Latin Kingdom

The fleet of the Fourth Crusade arrived at Constantinople in June of 1203. After a few days of preparation the attack was launched and the guard tower at Galata was captured. This allowed the Latins to lower the iron chain that guarded the entrance to the Golden Horn. Their fleet was able to enter the harbor and overwhelm the Roman naval opposition. A subsequent land attack failed to take the city, but the breakthrough of some Latin contingents caused Alexius III to flee the capital. The formerly deposed and blinded Isaac Angelus was reinstalled as emperor along with his son Alexius IV. Isaac stripped the city of everything valuable, but was unable to pay the huge demands of the Crusaders. In January of 1204, he and Alexius were murdered by the people of the city. Alexius Ducas was proclaimed the new emperor, but his reign lasted only until the 12th of April, 1204 when the Latins overwhelmed and sacked the city. For the next 57 years Constantinople was ruled by Latin emperors (also see page 156).

Latin Emperors of Constantinople

1204-5	Baldwin I of Flanders	
1206-16	Henry of Flanders	
1217	Peter of Courtenay	
1217-1219	Yolande	
1221-1228	Robert of Courtenay	
1228-1261	Baldwin II	
(1231-1237)	John de Brienne	

Bibliography — The Latin Kingdom

Bendall, Simon. "Latin Billon Trachea—Thessalonica or Constantinople?", *Numismatic Circular*, 92:3, 1984, p. 78.

Fotheringham, J.K. "Genoa and the Fourth Crusade", *The English Historical Review*, XXV, , 1910, pp. 20-57.

Laiou, A.E. *Constantinople and the Latins, the foreign policy of Andronicus II, 1282-1328*, Harvard, 1972.

Malloy, A., Irene Fraley Preston and A.J. Seltman. edited by Allen G. Berman. *Coins of the Crusader States 1098-1291*, New York, 1994.

Sear, David R., with the collaboration of Simon Bendall and Michael Dennis O'Hara. *Byzantine Coins and Their Values*, London, 1987, pp. 412-415.

The Politikon Coinage

Politikon, ca. AD 1320-1350
Billon tornese

The Politikon coinage struck at Constantinople, that is, the coinage bearing ΠΟΛΙΤΙΚΟΝ on its reverse, was a 14th century phenomenon. The word politikon is apparently a reference to coins of "the city". It is not certain for what purpose these coins were struck, and little has been written about them. They seem by their design and fabric to be associated with the Latin element which was powerful within certain enclaves of Constantinople in the 14th century. The coins fall into two main groups, those with imperial references and those struck anonymously. They are found in silver, billon and bronze of several denominations.

Although they are not dated, the earliest coins with imperial figures and names are attributed to the time of Andronicus III (ca. 1330). The latest are dated to the accession of Manuel II (1373). The anonymous types apparently circulated during this same period. These bear images like castle or city walls, keys, stars and crosses. All of the coins bear some variant of the inscription ΠΟΛΙΤΙΚΟΝ.

Even having suffered the humiliation of the Latin sack in 1204, and the yoke of Latin rule for more than half a century, it was impossible for the Romaion empire to escape contact with the West. The only way that rulers of the restored empire could avoid a repeat of the 1204 debacle was to align themselves with Western powers. This came at a price, and that price was preferential trade agreements. The outcome was that merchants in Constantinople lost their competitive edge, and the city itself was flooded with an influx of traders from Venice and Genoa. These Latin merchants and their families naturally congregated in homogeneous regions of the city. They built Latin churches and observed their normal customs. It is conceivable that the Politikon issues satisfied a need for coinage which suited their tastes and avoided distinctly Orthodox religious iconography. Whether this coinage was struck by the imperial mint, or some private mint within the city is uncertain.

The Final Days

The last Romaion coinage of Constantinople was that struck during the siege in 1453. Issued in the name of Constantine XI, this was an emergency coinage if ever there was one. For many years, numismatic treatises indicated that there were no coins struck for Constantine XI. In 1967, J.R. Jones published an interesting article in the *Numismatic Circular* titled "Literary Evidence for the Coinage of Constantine XI". Two observers at the scene during the siege, Nicolo Barbaro and Leonard of Chios, remarked that Constantine stripped gold and silver from the churches to mint coins to pay for the city's defense. Still, to that point no one had yet found a coin of that emperor.

In 1974, Simon Bendall published the discovery of a fractional silver coin of Constantine XI in the same journal. In the early 1990s a remarkable hoard of 91 coins of this emperor appeared on the ancient coin market. The denominations now known include the silver stavraton, 1/2 stavraton and 1/8 stavraton. They are crude in design and execution, and of poor metal quality, as emergency issues usually are.

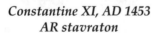

Constantine XI, AD 1453
AR stavraton

Constantine XI, AD 1453
AR 1/8 stavraton

Bibliography — Constantinople

Alexander, P.J. *The Patriarch Nicephorus of Constantinople*, Oxford, 1958.

Brown, H.F. The Venetians and the Venetian Quarter in Constantinople to the Close of the Twelfth Century", *Journal of Hellenic Studies*, XL, 1920, pp. 68-88.

Ebersolt, J. *Constantinople, Mélanges d'histoire et d'archéologie*, Paris, 1951.

Geanakoplos, D.J. *Constantinople and The West*, Univ. of Wisconsin, 1989.

Gilles, Pierre. tr. by John Ball. *The Antiquities of Constantinople*, first published 1729, reprint Italica Press, New York, 1988.

Hearsey, John. *City of Constantine*, London, 1963.

Jacobs, David. *Constantinople, City on the Golden Horn*, New York, 1969.

Liddell, Robert. *Byzantium and Istanbul*, London, 1958.

Cherson

Cherson was an ancient Greek city in the Crimea, at the northern end of the Black Sea. It was a commercial center, where the merchants from Constantinople conducted a flourishing trade. There, they exchanged textiles, jewelry and wine for furs, leather and slaves. It was also an alternate, but dangerous, route for carrying on the silk trade with China.

In the sixth century, Justinian built several forts and walls there to protect against the Huns. Being an "out of the way" place, Cherson was also a popular spot for exiling political enemies. Pope Martin had been exiled there, as had Justinian II. The city grew in importance and during the reign of Theophilus it was made the capital of a new theme under a military commander. In 989, Cherson was occupied by the Russian Prince Vladimir in order to force compliance with an earlier promise of the hand of princess Anna, sister of Basil II.

The bronze coinage of Cherson is particularly interesting in that some denominations were based on multiples of the pentanummium. A 20 nummi coin for example was indicated as 4 pentanummia. A 40 nummi coin was designated 8 pentanummia (see illustrations on page 11). As can be seen from the illustration below, the standard M=40 formula was also used. The obverse inscription is simply XЄPCШNOC or "Cherson".

Justin II and Sophia, AD 565-578, Cherson, AE 40 nummi

Bibliography — Cherson

Anoxin, B.A. *The coinage of Chersonesus IVth Century B.C. - XII Century A.D.*, BAR International Series 69, Oxford, 1980.

Golenko, Konstantin. "Gegenstempel auf Chersoner Münzen des Maurikios Tiberios", *Hamburger Beiträge zur Numismatik*, 6:18/19, pp. 5-12, 1964/1965.

Hahn, W. "The Numismatic History of Cherson in Early Byzantine Times", *Numismatic Circular*, 86:9, pp. 414-415 and 86:10, pp. 471-472 and 86:11, pp. 521-522, all in 1978.

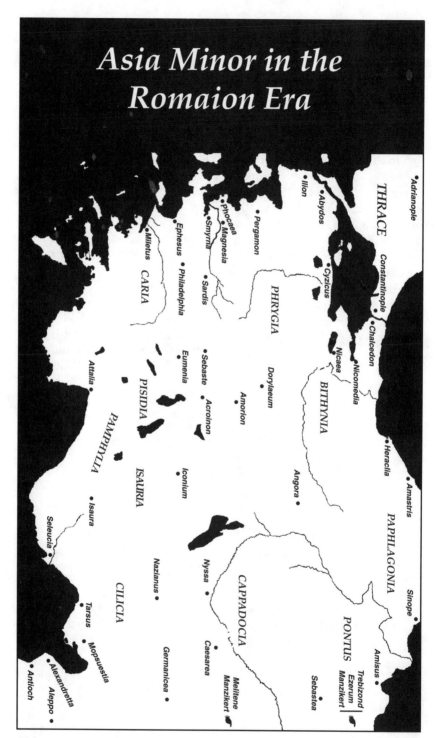

Asia Minor in the Romaion Era

Asia Minor

From the beginning of recorded time, and probably before, there has been a constant struggle between East and West for control of the lands known to us as Asia Minor or Anatolia. This is the region constituting the present day Republic of Turkey. The Romans began serious military operations in this region early in the first century BC under the leadership of Pompey the Great. It became a springboard for Eastern campaigns and saw a great many armies come and go. Sometimes their presence is recorded only by the coins struck there. Issues from the Seleucia Isauriae and Isaura mints, for example, reveal a brief Roman buildup during the reign of Heraclius. The Romans maintained control of the region, more or less, until the Battle of Manzikert in 1071. That famous battle, where the imperial army was routed and the emperor Romanus Diogenes himself was captured, marked the death knell for Romaion civilization and culture in the East.

The victory of Alp Arslan at Manzikert was followed by the establishment of a new Armenian kingdom in Cilicia. This small but resolute band of refugees carved out a new home in southeastern Asia Minor that remained under their control until late in the 14th century.

Asia Minor was always considered important real estate. It was not only a huge buffer zone for Rome, and later Constantinople, but a source of natural resources and wealth—including people. Over the course of a millennium, Asia Minor produced great numbers of soldiers, statesmen, philosophers and slaves for the empire. There were literally hundreds of small cities within Asia Minor, but history has left their story untold. They did not disappear with the Romans, they were simply assimilated into a new empire. Over time, the ethnicity of the region changed but the traditions were not forgotten, and change was usually gradual and relatively peaceful. Generally speaking, the Muslim invaders of Asia Minor—at first Arabs and later Turks—were tolerant masters. A traveller to modern Turkey cannot help but notice that many place-names are simply Turkish variants of their original Greek or Roman names, e.g. Sinop for Sinope, Trabzon for Trebizond, Kayseri for Caesarea, Anavarza for Anazarbus, Iznik for Nicaea etc.

During the Latin episode in the 13th century, Romaion aristocrats fled Constantinople and established themselves in the outlying areas of Greece and Asia Minor. The new capital of the "Vichy" empire became Nicaea, in northwest Anatolia. From here the rebuilding of imperial power was undertaken. A competitor for this honor was the independent empire of Trebizond. Established in 1204 by a grandson of Andronicus I, it also became a port for refugees. Even after the empire at Constantinople had been restored, Trebizond maintained its independence. In fact, it survived eight years longer than the city of Constantinople itself.

Nicaea was founded about 300 BC by Antigonus, one of the successors of Alexander the Great. It was located on the eastern shore of Lake Ascania in what is now northwestern Turkey. Shortly after, it was taken by Lysimachos, and named in honor of his wife. The city was built on flat ground, and had great double walls, which still exist. It was one of the chief cities of the province of Asia under the early Romans. Later, it became an important Christian center and eventually it served the tattered refugees of Constantinople as a seat of government in exile.

Theodore I Comnenus-Lascaris, AD 1208-1222
AR trachy, Magnesia mint

Our interest is limited here to the period from 1204 to 1261. Immediately after the fall of the capital, refugees poured into Nicaea, which became one of the main staging points for recovery. Theodore Lascaris emerged as the leader of this growing band and he set about rebuilding an empire from nothing. In 1208, a new Patriarch was chosen and Theodore was crowned the legitimate successor to Constantine XI. Fourteen years later, when Theodore's successor came to the throne he inherited a secure, growing and determined empire.

John III Ducas-Vatatzes. AD 1222-1254
AV hyperpyron, Magnesia mint

John Ducas-Vatatzes (John III) was the son-in-law of Theodore Lascaris. His reign of 32 years was perhaps the most productive in the annals of imperial history. It was the rebuilding of Romaion society, preservation of its culture and consolidation of its resources that became John's lot. He was a patient ruler, foregoing an attack on Constantinople to concentrate on the task at hand. Through his effort, the Romaioi in Greece and Asia Minor were united and able to put pressure on the Latins from both sides.

John's son, Theodore II Ducas-Lascaris was a man of great ability and learning, but his reign was plagued by discontent among the aris-

Theodore II Ducas-Lascaris
AD 1254-1258
Billon trachy, Magnesia mint

tocracy. When he died after only four years, his son (John IV) was still a minor. The resulting power struggle saw the end of the Lascarid dynasty and the rise of the Palaeologids under their progenitor Michael VIII. This new and powerful dynasty was to rule Nicaea and the recovered capital of Constantinople until its fall in 1453.

Coins of the empire of Nicaea were struck at the nearby mint in Magnesia—a city of some consequence in Greek and early Roman times. Following the capture of Thessalonica by John III, the mint at that city also struck coins for the Nicaean emperor. The bulk of these issues were billon trachy coins, but a few types of the hyperpyron and tetarteron are known.

In 1261, the army of Michael VIII recaptured Constantinople and the emperor in exile reclaimed his throne on the Bosphorus. As history has recorded, it was to be a bittersweet victory. The next two centuries were to the people of Constantinople what the fifth century was to the people of Rome.

For more information about the Empire of Nicaea see pages 105-107 and 181-183.

Bibliography — Nicaea

Angold, M. *A Byzantine government in exile. Government and society under the Laskarids of Nicaea, 1204-1261*, London, 1975.

Gardner, A. *The Lascarids of Nicaea, The Story of an Empire in Exile*, London, 1912 (outdated).

Miller, W. "The Emperor of Nicaea and the Recovery of Constantinople", *Cambridge Medieval History* IV, 1923, pp. 478-516.

Veglery A. and A. Millas. "Rare Copper Coins of the Laskarids (1204-1261) and Palaeologids (1258-1453)", *Numismatic Circular*, 85:3, 1977, pp. 94-96 and 85:4, pp. 142-144.

Wroth, W. *Catalogue of the Coins of the Vandals, Ostrogoths and Lombards and of the Empires of Thessalonica, Nicaea and Trebizond in the British Museum*, London, 1911, (1966 Argonaut reprint as *Western and Provincial Byzantine Coins in the British Museum*).

Trebizond had long been an imperial city, and before that a Roman city, and before that Greek—going back to the 8th century BC. Because of its extremely good fortifications, it was one of the few places in Asia Minor that held out against the Turks after Manzikert. In 1092, Theodore Gabras claimed the city and for six years ruled it independently from Constantinople. Its history between that time and the beginning of the 13th century is obscure.

The "Empire of Trebizond" arose shortly before the fall of Constantinople when Alexius and David Comnenus (grandsons of Andronicus I, Comnenus) captured the city with the help of Queen Thamar of Georgia. Due to the Latin preoccupation with the Bulgarians and Romaioi in the Balkans, the Comneni at Trebizond were able to expand without serious opposition.

Manuel I Comnenus
AD 1238-1263, AR Asper

A long line of emperors issued coins from this city and they are fairly well documented due to efforts of several modern numismatists (see the bibliography on facing page). The history of Trebizond is really the history of a feudal outpost. It managed to survive, almost in isolation, while the rest of Asia Minor was falling to the Turks. Only a few of the Trebizond coins are illustrated here as a sampler of what is available. A complete list of emperors and coin types is available in Sear, *Byzantine Coins and Their Values.*

John II
AD 1280-1297, AR Asper

Theodora, older sister of John II
ca. AD 1285, AR Asper

Alexius II
AD 1297-1330, AR Asper

Basil
AD 1332-1340, AR Asper

Bendall, Simon. "Trebizond issued independent series of bronzes", *The Celator*, 03:04, April 1989, pp. 1ff.

___. " A Follis of Alexius I of Trebizond", *Numismatic Circular*, 89:7-8, 1981, p. 237.

___. "Andronicus I of Trebizond", *Numismatic Circular* LXXXVIII, 1980, pp. 400-401.

___. "The Coinage of Trebizond under Isaac II (A.D. 1185-95), with a Note on an Unfinished Byzantine Die", *ANSMN* 24, 1979, pp. 213-17.

___. "Some further notes on the mint of Trebizond under Alexius I", *Numismatic Chronicle*, 1979, p. 211.

___. "The Mint of Trebizond under Alexius I and the Gabrades", *Numismatic Chronicle*, 1977, pp. 126-36.

Bryer, A.A.M. "A Byzantine Family: The Gabrades, ca. 979-c. 1653", *The University of Birmingham Historical Journal* 12, 1970, pp. 164-87.

___. "Trebizond: The Last Byzantine Empire", *History Today*, 10:2, 1960, pp. 125-135.

Gordus A.A. and D.M. Metcalf. "Non-destructive chemical analysis of the Byzantine silver coinage of Trebizond", *Arkheion Pontou* XXXIII, 1975/6, pp. 28-35.

Kursanskis, Michael. "Monnaies divisionnaires en argent de l'Empire de Trebizonde", *Revue numismatique,* 1977, pp. 103-108.

Metcalf, D.M. and I.T. Roper. "A Hoard of Copper Trachea of Andronicus I of Trebizond (1222-1235)", *Numismatic Circular* 83, June 1975, pp. 237-38.

Miller, W. *Trebizond, the Last Greek Empire,* Chicago, 1969.

Retowski, O. *Die Münzen des Komnenen von Trapezunt,* Moscow, 1910 (Braunschweig, 1974 reprint).

Toumanoff, C. "On the Relationship Between the Founder of the Empire of Trebizond and the Georgian Queen Thamara", *Speculum,* 15:3, 1940, p. 299ff.

Vasiliev, A. "The foundation of the Empire of Trebizond", *Speculum* XI, 1936, pp. 3-37.

Veglery A. and A. Millas. "Copper Coins of Andronicus I, Comnenus Gidon (1222-1235)", *Numismatic Circular* 85, Nov. 1977, pp. 487-88.

Wroth, W. *Catalogue of the Coins of the Vandals, Ostrogoths and Lombards and of the Empires of Thessalonica, Nicaea and Trebizond in the British Museum,* London, 1911, (1966 Argonaut reprint as *Western and Provincial Byzantine Coins in the British Museum).*

Seleucia Isauriae and Isaura

The mints of Seleucia Isauriae and Isaura were active only for a short time during the reign of Heraclius. Their main purpose was to support the emperor's expeditions against the Sasanians. Both mints were located in the southeast of Asia Minor, with Seleucia Isauriae being a major port city (Seleucia ad Calycadnum, or modern day Silifke) and Isaura located a bit to the north in the Taurus mountains. Both cities struck coins during the earlier Roman period, and before that were known as hideouts for the notorious pirates of Cilicia.

Heraclius, Seleucia Isauriae mint
AE 40 nummi, AD 616/17

Heraclius, Isaura mint
AE 40 nummi, AD 617/18

Seleucia Isauriae was active from 615 to 618, with at least 5 officinae. Isaura apparently had only one officina producing coinage, in 618, after the closing of the Seleucia Isauriae mint.

The coinage of both cities is quite scarce. Harlan J. Berk has identified three celators who engraved dies for essentially all of the coins struck at these two mints. The first two worked only at Seleucia Isauriae and the third worked at both mints. All of the coins issued at these mints were crudely overstruck on earlier issues.

Bibliography — Seleucia Isauriae and Isaura

Berk, Harlan. "The three celators of Seleucia and Isauriae", *The Celator*, 07:08, August 1993, p. 8.

___. *Eastern Roman Successors of the Sestertius*, Joliet, IL, 1986, No. 574-579.

Grierson, P. "The Isaurian Coins of Heraclius", *Numismatic Chronicle*, 1951, pp. 56-67.

Sear, David R. *Byzantine Coins and Their Values*, London, 1987, pp. 181-182.

Whitting, P.D. *Byzantine Coins*, London, 1973, p. 132.

The earliest coin bearing Armenian letters was struck by one Kiurke II Curopalatus (1048-1100), who ruled at Lori in northeastern Armenia. It is a very rare bronze coin, not only because of its attribution, but also because it is copied after the "Byzantine" anonymous follis of John Tzimisces (Class A1).

Kiurke II, AD 1048-11
AE follis, Lori, Armenia

Roupen I, AD 1080-1095
AE Pogh, Cilician Armenia

The Armenians began migrating out of Greater Armenia after the fall of their capital of Ani in 1064. They were caught between the Romans in the West and the Turks in the East and were hard pressed to find a piece of land in which to settle. Cilicia, which had in earlier times been an incredibly rich agricultural region had suffered from its rivers silting up and much of the land had become marshy and malaria infested. Consequently, the region was not heavily populated. Many Armenians had already migrated here before Roupen I declared an independent kingdom here in 1080.

The coinage of Cilician Armenia is rich in diversity and at least some varieties are plentiful. Although the Armenians were not in any way a part of the Romaion people, the two cultures were inexorably entwined for hundreds of years. We find one emperor from Constantinople waging war on the Armenians and another legitimizing their empire by crowning their king. They were at times allies and at other times enemies. But then this is a common malady of civilizations in general.

Bibliography — Armenia

Bedoukian, Paul Z. "A Hoard of Bilingual Trams of Hetoum I of Cilician Armenia", *ANSMN* 23, 1978, pp. 149-160.

___. *Coinage of Cilician Armenia*, ANS NNM 147, 1962.

Nercessian, Y.T. *Armenian Coins and Their Values*, Los Angeles, 1995.

Nersessian, Sirarpie der. *Armenia and the Byzantine Empire*, Cambridge, Massachusetts, 1945.

Saryan, L.A. "Careful searching leads to opportunities in the acquisition of rare Armenian coins", *The Celator*, 06:07, July 1992, pp. 40-41.

Cyprus

Very few coins were struck on the island of Cyprus during the centuries dealt with here. A mint was apparently located at the ancient city of Salamis, which had been renamed Constantia. During the uprising

Revolt of the Heraclii, AD 608-610
AE 40 nummi, Cyprus

of Heraclius the Exarch of Carthage, and his son, a small group of coins were struck there. These bore the standard consular bust imagery for which they are known. Heraclius also struck coins there after he had been crowned emperor but the duration was brief. The mint was reopened by Constantine IV to countermark coins previously issued by Constans II.

Isaac Comnenus
AD 1184-1191, AE tetarteron

The bulk of the imperial coinage from Cyprus was issued by Isaac Comnenus. These consist of electrum and billon trachea and bronze tetartera. The story of Isaac and his "empire" on the island of Cyprus reads like a movie script. For more on that see page 101. The impetuous Isaac lost the island to Richard, Coeur de Lion. Since Constantinople failed to intervene, it was also lost permanently as a part of the empire.

Bibliography — Cyprus

Bendall, Simon. "Isaac Comnenus: just a little empire on Cyprus", *The Celator,* 03:02, February 1989, p. 1ff.

Dikigoropoulos, J. "A Byzantine Hoard from Kharcha, Cyprus, *Numismatic Chronicle,* 1956, pp. 255-265.

Donald, P.J. and P.D. Whitting. "A hoard of trachea of John II and Manuel I from Cyprus", *Mints, dies and currency. Essays in memory of Albert Baldwin,* London, 1971, pp. 75-84.

Metcalf, D.M. "A follis of Isaac Comnenus of Cyprus, 1184-91, from the di Cesnola collection", *Seaby Coin and Medal Bulletin,* 1975, pp. 261-262.

Antioch

Antioch, from the day of its founding in the third century BC, was an emporium for East-West trade. Its location was perfectly suited to a gathering of traders from every direction. It was also a popular attraction for usurpers, conquerors, religious zealots and would-be land barons of every description. The city changed hands like changes in the weather. The Roman mint was only operational from about AD 512 to 610.

Antioch was renamed Theoupolis after its devastation by an earthquake in AD 528. From that time on the mint name is recorded as THЄUP or some variant. Consequently, during the reign of Justinian coins were issued from this city in both names. The coins struck with the mint mark ANT, struck only from 527 to 528/9 are much less common.

Justinian I, AE 40 nummi Antioch

Justinian I, AE 40 nummi, Antioch as Theoupolis

Bibliography — Antioch

Downey, G. *History of Antioch in Syria from Seleucus to the Arab Conquest*, Princeton, 1961.

Grierson, P. "The Monograms on Late Sixth-Century Pentanummia of Antioch", *Numismatic Circular*, 83:1, 1975, p. 5. followed and updated by Bendall and Roper "Late Sixth-Century Monogram Pentanummia" in 83:2, 1975, p. 55.

Kent, J.P.C. "The Antiochene Coinage of Tiberius Constantine and Maurice, 578-602", *Numismatic Chronicle*, 1959, pp. 99-103.

Prawdzic-Golemberski, E.J. and D.M. Metcalf. "The circulation of Byzantine coins on the south-eastern frontiers of the Empire", *Numismatic Chronicle*, 1963, pp. 83-92.

Waage, Dorothy B. *Antioch-on-the-Orontes, IV, pt. 2. Greek, Roman, Byzantine and Crusaders' Coins*, Princeton, 1952.

Until recently, it was thought that Heraclius was the only Romaion emperor to strike coins in Jerusalem. Now, a solidus of Phocas has also been assigned here. In any case, the surviving specimens from this mint are very rare.

It would seem that the Heraclius folles are closely related, and perhaps share an obverse die. The dating of the bronze coins (only struck in year 4) has been interpreted both as a regnal date (AD 613/4) and an indictional date (AD 630/31). Emotionally, and perhaps historically, the latter date is popular because it follows closely on the return of Heraclius to Jerusalem with the

Heraclius, AV solidus, AD 613/14

Heraclius, AE follis, AD 613/14
XC NIKA in exergue

Heraclius, AE follis, AD 613/14
IЄPOCO in exergue

True Cross which had been recovered from the Persians. Of course the same argument could be used to explain the striking of coins at Jerusalem early in his campaign as a form of inspiration, motivation or propaganda—not to mention fiscal necessity. The fabric and style of these coins seems to fit better with the early issues of Heraclius than with the later, and the word ANNO preceding the numerals tends to argue, however slightly, for a regnal date rather than an indictional one.

A series of gold coins previously attributed to Alexandria (see illustration above) are now thought to be from Jerusalem and are also dated to AD 613/14 .

Alexandria

After Justinian closed the Academy in Athens (529) Alexandria became the center of Aristotelian and Platonic study, with schools remaining open into the eighth century. It was a center of Christian ideology as well, and was often in conflict with the thinking of church leaders at the capital and in Asia Minor.

Justinian I, AD 527-565
AE 33 nummi, Alexandria

Alexandria was important to Constantinople, and the rest of the empire, as a major source of grain from Egypt. It prospered as long as the imperial navy maintained its supremacy. However, the city became increasingly difficult to defend in the seventh century as first the Persians, and later the Arabs, swept over Egypt. The Roman army was finally defeated in 636 and the entire region was lost. This should not be taken to mean that Romaion contact with Egypt ceased to exist. Initially, the only thing that really changed was the purse which held the taxes and tributes. Trade between Egypt and Constantinople continued, and many Christians, known as Copts, stayed in Egypt after its fall to the Arabs.

As early as the days of Augustus, the coins struck in Alexandria were unique in style, denomination and composition. This individuality continued for as long as Roman coins were struck there. Note, for example, the introduction of a 12 nummi coin under Justin I, to be followed by sporadic striking of 33, 6, and 3 nummi pieces under Justinian and later rulers. Ironically, the 12 nummi coins look and feel very much like the potin tetradrachms of three centuries earlier.

Bibliography — Alexandria

Bendall, Simon. "A Hoard of Heraclian Six-Nummi Coins of Alexandria", *Numismatic Circular*, 88:12, 1980, p. 441.

Johnson, Allen C. and Louis C. West. *Byzantine Egypt: Economic studies*, Princeton, 1949.

Phillips, J.R. "The Byzantine bronze coins of Alexandria in the seventh century", *Numismatic Chronicle*, 1962, pp. 225-241.

West, Louis C. & Allan C. Johnson. *Currency in Roman and Byzantine Egypt*, Princeton, 1944.

Carthage

The province of Africa was captured from the Vandal king Gelimer by Justinian's general Belisarius in 533/34. A mint seems to have been activated shortly thereafter. Maurice Tiberius, who came to the throne in 582, rebuilt the city into a strongly fortified military outpost. He appointed a special governor, called an Exarch, who was in charge of the military and civil branches. Later, the revolt against Phocas was nurtured in Carthage where the Exarch Heraclius reigned with a fair amount of autonomy. From the reign of Justinian until the Arab conquest (698) the Carthage mint produced a broad and interesting, if sporadic, series of coins—many of which are scarce.

It was probably the most important mint in the west, having only Syracuse as a potential competitor. Aside from the mint marks, which are fairly straightforward, coins from Carthage have their own distinctive fabric. They are typically rather thick coins with rounded edges. Reverses sometimes have a characteristic border with a wreath and inner circle. An unusual issue of Justin II and Sophia includes the unusual acclamation "Vita" (giver of life?) in the obverse formula. Gold coins were very small in diameter and thick in comparison to the same denominations at other mints.

Justin II and Sophia, AD 565-578
AE 40 nummi, Carthage mint
(Rare variant with "Bita" instead of Vita)

In 695, when the Arabs first occupied Carthage, the mint was relocated to Sardinia. The last ruler striking coins with Carthage mintmarks was Anastasius II (713-715), but these actually would have been struck at the new site.

Bibliography — Carthage

Fairhead, N. "Some Interesting Silver and Bronze Coins of Maurice Tiberius of Carthage", *Num. Circ.*, 89:12, 1981, pp. 398-99; and, "Some Pentanummia of Justinian I of Carthage", *Num. Circ.*, 87:7-8, 1979, p. 342.

Grierson, P. "A Byzantine Hoard from North Africa", *Numismatic Chronicle*, 1953, pp. 146-8.

Morrison, Cécile. "Carthage: The Moneta Auri under Justinian I and Justin II, 537-578", Hahn & Metcalf, ed., *Studies in Early Byzantine Gold Coinage*, ANSNS 17, New York, 1988, pp. 41-64.

Whitting, P.D. "A Seventh-Century Hoard at Carthage", *Numismatic Chronicle*, 1966, pp. 225-233.

Imitative Issues

by Peter Lampinen

Although the word *Byzantine* has become a synonym for intricacy, intrigue and decadence, the Byzantine empire survived for some 1000 years—a remarkable feat of longevity. Looking at it from a numismatic viewpoint, one can find examples of similar endurance. The gold solidus, introduced by Constantine I, was a firm anchor for the Byzantine economy for over 600 years until replaced by the histamenon and later the hyperpyron. The bronze follis, an innovation of Anastasius I, enjoyed a more roller coaster existence, but nonetheless circulated in its various forms until the reforms of Alexius I in 1092. By comparison the earlier Roman aureus and sestertius lasted barely 300 years in active use. The Byzantine coinage system was an obvious success over its long lifetime, fulfilling the requirements of providing a store of value and an adequate supply of useful circulating currency.

Any successful enterprise encourages competitors and imitators; a successful coinage system is no exception. It is a truism that the best way to make money is to make it yourself. A widespread and well regarded coinage system will attract followers wishing to capitalize on its success. Imitations of the mainstays of the Byzantine system, the solidus and follis, probably appeared shortly after the introduction of the original types. Some of these imitations were certainly meant to deceive with criminal intent, such as counterfeit solidi and other gold coins seen in any age, the plated examples known as fourrees and often objects of study in themselves. However, in this section we shall deal not with counterfeits in the traditional sense of the word, but rather with a broader class of imitations— those intended to replace or extend the regular currency.

As the term (rightly or not) is known and used by many historians, the Byzantine period begins in the mid 4th century, proceeding from the reign of Constantine. If one word could be used to describe the following thousand year history of the eastern empire, that word would probably be transition. As the classical Mediterranean world was superseded by the eastern Christian empire and later European nation states the Byzantine imperium was subjected to various, often divergent impulses. On the one hand, its territory shrank under continual pressures applied by both external and internal forces, with Goths, Franks, Slavs, Persians, Arabs, Crusaders, Turks and other external foes lopping off bits of the empire, while internal intrigues led to nominal autonomy in regions of the remaining territory. In opposition to this diminuation of geographic and political hegemony, the cultural and economic influence of Byzantium was felt far beyond its borders. While the reality on the ground might be disintegration and chaos, the conception of an immortal and omnipotent empire still held strong in many minds. Thus for both external foe and internal separatist it was vital to retain some tangible connection with the imperial center. This might be art, architecture, court ritual or, of direct interest to the common man, the coinage. The opponents and successors of the empire, many without a coinage tradition of their own and often despite deeply held antipathy towards the Byzantines, would employ traditional types and standards for the coins struck in their newly won lands.

The Western Empire and pseudo-imperial offshoots

Germanic imitation of a gold solidus of Valens

Any discussion of Byzantine imitation coinage has to begin in the pre-Byzantine period, numismatically speaking. By the last quarter of the 4th century Gothic tribes from the steppes and forests beyond the imperial frontiers had deeply impacted the Roman world, and were in turn influenced by classical culture. The northern tribesmen had little use for coinage until they settled within the boundaries of the empire and began to aspire to own those things which could be bought with silver and gold, in convenient form, acceptable to the local population. Production of "pseudo-imperial" issues began shortly thereafter. The first issues bore no evidence of an autonomous striking authority, being straightforward imitations of more or less standard fineness. The only visible factor distinguishing them from the originals is a certain naive quality to the workmanship, which eventually mutates into a distinctive regional or national style as the different cultures begin to diverge. Of course, categorizing coins on a stylistic basis can be troublesome when styles are in flux and subject to the whims and variable abilities of perhaps not highly experienced engravers. A solidus of "Valens" can be identified as an imitation by the somewhat loose obverse portrait, but the reverse die seems to be a regular issue of Trier. Is this a "semi-Germanic" solidus, or the product of two engravers reproducing the official solidus with varying degrees of aptitude? To go beyond the basic question of official versus imitation and try to resolve the problem of place of striking would require a remarkable confluence of historical and archaeological data, often lacking. Many of these anonymous imitations of the 4th and 5th centuries must be labeled "Germanic" or "Gothic" without further specification.

One of the earliest tribes to forge a distinct national identity was the Vandals, an identity strengthened during their long trek across Europe, through Roman territory into Spain and finally, in 429, across the Straits of Gibraltar into north Africa. Silver siliquae of "Honorius" have been attributed to the early Vandal rulers, but by the reign of Gunthamund (484-496) a distinct national coinage in silver and bronze was introduced. The most com-

Vandalic silver siliqua in the name of Honorius

mon bronze coins found are nummi of Thrasamund (496-523) which copy the common late Roman running Victory type, although Victory may resemble a haystack more than anything else. An interesting innovation of the Vandals was the autonomous civic bronzes of Carthage, where a large bronze coin of 42 nummi value circulated some 20 years prior to the introduction of Anastasius' follis in 498.

A similar large bronze coin appears in Ostrogothic Rome at about the same time. Ostrogothic coinage in silver and bronze bear distinctive civic and royal types and deserve to be discussed under the heading of early medieval coinage rather than mere Byzantine imitations. The gold, however, remained conservative, preserving the types of imperial solidi and tremisses until the end of the Ostrogothic kingdom. Their last king, Theia, fell before imperial armies in 553. An Italian style is recognizable, with low relief and static portraiture, with one frequent local variation, a six pointed star in the reverse field, as opposed to the typical eight-pointed star found at Constantinople.

The reconquest of Italy by Justinian did not long outlast him. By 568 the north of Italy was in the hands of another group, the Lombards. Although a unique style of broad flan tremisses appeared under Lombard rule by the beginning of the 7th century, their earliest coinage consisted of close imita-

Lombardic AR half siliqua in the name of Justinian I

tions of tremisses and siliquae of Justinian—not always easily separated from imperial issues. Imitations of silver Byzantine coins were for the most part restricted to Italy, where silver played a more important role in daily life. The circulation of silver hexagrams and later miliaresia from Constantinople was too sporadic to encourage much copying. Ostrogothic and Lombard siliquae would preserve a tradition of silver coinage that would later develop into the Merovingian denier and spread throughout western Europe.

No such tradition of silver coinage took root in the last Gothic kingdom, the Visigoths of southern France and Spain. Gold solidi imitating issues of Ravenna are recognized as products of a mint at the Visigothic capital of Toulouse before 507, when the Frankish king Clovis pushed the Visigoths south into Iberia. The Visigothic gold coinage from that point onward consisted solely of tremisses, struck at various Spanish mints in the name of Anastasius, Justin I and Justinian until the reign of Leovigild (568-586), who initiated the regal Visigothic series. The Visigothic renditions developed their own wonderful unique style, with the curious "grasshopper" Victory on the reverse. Until recently it was assumed the Visigoths struck only gold coinage, but by the mid-1980's a number of bronze nummi came to be recognized as autonomous civic issues, bearing the monograms not of kings but of Spanish mints such as Emerita and Toledo. Prior to this identification such types had been regarded as mere poor copies of late Roman and Byzantine imperial monogram nummi. Although still regarded as rare, the more common types of these nummi are readily available. Nonetheless, many varieties are truly scarce, and new types continue to be found, including several examples of bronze multiples.

This brief survey of Byzantine imitative coinage in the west has to restrict itself to the very beginnings of western coinage within the tribes and regions that in time became the nation states of modern Europe. The Byzantines retained a foothold in the west, in Sicily and southern Italy, and Byzantine influence is still to be found in the early issues of the Italian city-states such as Beneventum, Naples and Salerno [see the section "Sicily / Italy" on pages 125-6]. Some of the latest direct imitations of Byzantine coins come from Sicily, where solidi in the name of Theophilus were struck by the Arab conquerors of the island. That conquest completed in 902. In later centuries, "bezant" became a generic term for a gold coin around the Mediterranean.

The Balkans

Crude Balkan imitation of a follis of Anastasius I

The mountainous Balkan peninsula formed the hinterlands for the cosmopolitan city of Constantinople. It formed an important node in the Byzantine trading network with Europe, represented a fertile ground for religious and cultural proselytizing and excelled as a never-ending source of anxiety, alarm and catastrophe for Byzantine rulers. With all these facets, the Balkans had to present numerous opportunities for imitators of Byzantine coinage. Gold and bronze counterfeits saw widespread circulation in the 6th century Balkans communities on the edges of the empire, most of which cannot be attributed to a specific region or group, but the best of which have a certain charm of their own—being in style very similar to the best of modern refrigerator art in finger-painting and crayon. The bronze follis introduced by Anastasius seems to have been especially popular; numerous examples can be found of folles copied from the prototypes of Anastasius, Justin I and Justinian.

These follis imitations fade away at about the time of the arrival of two new groups of invaders, the Central Asian Slavs and the Turkic Avars. By the 580's both groups presented a serious threat to imperial foundations. One of the most chaotic and dangerous periods of Byzantine history was sparked by the Avar intrusion. The emperor Maurice Tiberius was overthrown and murdered by rebellious army units sent to fight the Avars in 602, and the next forty years would see the empire almost crumble in the face of civil war and multiple foreign invasions. The situation might have been nightmarish for the Byzantines, but for the numismatist interested in the exchange and adaptation of coin types it is a very fertile period for study.

A number of intriguing copies of solidi of the 6th-7th centuries are found in modern Bulgaria, Rumania and Hungary that have been attributed to the Avars and to a lesser degree the Slavs. These range from good quality, full weight and fineness imitations to pale gold or even silver tribal adaptations of Byzantine types. Examples of thin gold uniface "bracteates" have also been found in the region. This first phase of

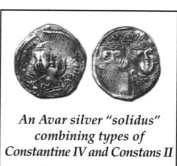

An Avar silver "solidus" combining types of Constantine IV and Constans II

Balkans imitative coinage probably came to an end in the mid-7th century. Although the Avars were strong enough to besiege Constantinople in 626, their power was broken a few decades later under pressure from further wandering tribes, who would in later years coalesce into the medieval Bulgars, Croats and Serbs. At the same time the Balkan peoples were laying the foundations of their medieval states, the Byzantine empire was mired in confusion, verging on implosion. Its sporadic and often pitiful coinage does not appear to have inspired the production of many imitations, other than the occasional fourree solidus. Crude, lightweight specimens of many types of 9th and 10th century folles are frequently encountered, but many scholars regard these as the products of Byzantine branch mints in Greece, perhaps at Thessalonica.

The second phase of Balkan coinage production goes into high gear with the introduction of the anonymous follis series during the reign of John I (969-976). The explicit Christian imagery must have struck a chord with the recently converted Balkan masses, because the official mint is-

Anonymous follis of Class A with retrograde legends. Imitation, or a bad day at the mint?

sues were accompanied by a fair quantity of copies, to meet excess demand no doubt. These Christian images would also be the prototypes for the initial coinage of several medieval Christian states, such as the first Crusader issues of Edessa and Antioch, medieval Armenia and distant Georgia in the Caucasus.

A third and final phase of imitative coinage begins in the 12th cen-

A Bulgarian trachy imitating Manuel I. The flan, originally much broader, has been cut down and silvered

tury, after the introduction of the billon aspron trachy by Alexius I in 1092. By this time the Bulgarians have established a secure basis for their kingdom, and the need for a functional national coinage became apparent. Passable imitations of the Byzantine trachy were as good a starting point as any. And we now step into one of the most complicated problems in Byzantine numismatics. The original trachea of John II, Manuel I, Andronicus I and Isaac II were some of the most poorly struck, over designed examples of Byzantine coinage ever produced. To add to that the problem of trying to separate out even worse Bulgarian imitations means testing the limits of modern numismatic scholarship. M.F. Hendy and D.M. Metcalf have both conducted extensive analyses of Balkan hoards and coinage systems to elucidate this complex intertwined series, occasionally coming to completely different conclusions. It will suffice to say that the Bulgarian imitative trachea are generally consid-

ered to have a smaller design area than the official issues and are less accurate in addressing the details of imperial court costume, which the Byzantines took great pains to depict.

By the time of Constantine Asen (1257-1277) a clear national Bulgarian coinage has evolved, one

Bulgaria, trachy of Constantine Asen, king enthroned / cross

still heavily influenced by the empire on its borders. That empire would continue to influence the coinage of countries far beyond its physical borders, as wars, trade and the spread of Orthodox Christianity brought many peoples into contact with Byzantine culture. Traces of Byzantine stylistic heritage can be seen on the early coinage of Serbia, Hungary, Trebizond, Ukraine, Russia and even Denmark—a heritage that outlasted the empire.

Georgian imitation of a Trebizond asper

A few problems in identification

Each branch mint striking coinage in the 6th century Byzantine empire soon developed its own distinct style. For example, the half folles of Maurice Tiberius, which often bear no mintmark, can usually be readily separated into the issues of the Constantinople, Nicomedia or Cyzicus mints on the basis of style. That is why numismatists readily recognized a series that did not fit the pattern of normal mint issues. These coins, folles and half folles of Justin II, Tiberius II and Maurice are clearly marked as issues of Thessalonica, Constantinople, Nicomedia, Cyzicus and Antioch, but are just as obviously not products of these mints, but rather of a common origin. Portraiture is rather broad, with Justin and his wife looking somewhat like mummies and Tiberius and Maurice moon-faced. Lettering is stiffer and more block-like, when compared to the originals, and the planchets appear grainy, with sharply defined edges. W. Hahn was the first to call them "moneta militaris imitativa", although others before him had suggested an *ad hoc* traveling military mint as the source of these imitations. They are stylistically identical to half folles of the Rome mint, and an Italian origin has been postulated, perhaps to supply troops sent to oppose incursions into the

"MMI" half follis of Justin II, imitating a Constantinople mint issue

"MMI" follis of Justin II, imitating a Cyzicus mint issue

155

Italian province still only precariously held by the Byzantines. MMI coins have been found in many regions of the empire, and the precise origin and function of these imitations still remains to be resolved.

Latin Kingdom, Billon Trachy, AD 1204-1261

Of all the catastrophies to befall Byzantium, the cruelest and most unnecessary had to be the "Great Betrayal" of 1204. Armies of the Fourth Crusade, sent eastward to fight the Muslims for possession of the Holyland, were diverted by greed and Italian agents jealous of Byzantine control of Mediterranean trade routes. Instead, they set upon the destruction of a fellow Christian kingdom (see page 132). The Latin Christian kingdom in Constantinople would last until 1261 under rulers dominated by the western powers. Contemporary records refer to coins struck by the Latin kings, but until the 1960's the exact nature of this coinage could not be untangled from the myriad miserable billon and bronze trachea of the period—Byzantine, Bulgarian and Latin all mixed together. M.F. Hendy is to be credited with the first comprehensive analysis of this series, and now some 23 classes have been identified from Constantinople, with others found at Thessalonica, held by the Latins until 1224. Many of these trachea combine types familiar from previous Byzantine issues, but others, such as the "Saints Peter and Paul" type are unique to the Latin series. Some complications still remain, however, for there is a parallel series of small module pieces that resemble the Latin trachea. Are these branch mint issues or imitations, essentially imitations of imitations?

Egypt

Egypt deserves a heading of its own. In a form of ancient numismatic apartheid that Roman province had possessed a distinct coinage system since Augustan times (see page 147), and the closed economic system that produced this coinage also sprouted distinctive local copies. Egypt had been drawn into the imperial coinage system with the

Cast imitation of a nummus of Marcian, from Egypt. Note the casting sprue on the edge.

reforms of Diocletian, but still suffered from periodic coin shortages. The situation seems to have been most dire in the 5th century, when the amount of small bronze nummi in circulation proved insufficient for the Egyptian economy. The locals made do with a plethora of cast imitations, starting out with reasonably good cast copies of official nummi, but after several generations of copying copies ended up with cast blank discs with no trace of the original. These imitation nummi survive up to the reign of Justinian, and quantities of them appear not only at sites in Egypt but all along the eastern Mediterranean coast into Palestine and Syria. At certain times and places the copies outnumber the originals and overall represent a significant percentage of the circulating currency.

Egypt's special needs were met with the special coinage discussed earlier. All of the circulating denominations would be copied, but the 12 nummi was the workhorse of the economy and the most frequently imitated. The officially struck 12 nummi weighed about 3 to 6 grams, but cast imitations are found—naming Justinian when legible—that weigh about 1 gram and reduce down in size to the lightest locally struck nummus, about 0.2 grams. Sometime around the end of the 6th century a new class of imitation appears, on a struck flan weighing about 2 grams—the legend, when visible, being gibberish. These have

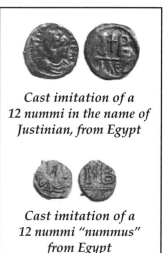

Cast imitation of a 12 nummi in the name of Justinian, from Egypt

Cast imitation of a 12 nummi "nummus" from Egypt

been catalogued in the Dumbarton Oaks catalogue as issues of Phocas, but it seems unlikely they should be restricted to a specific reign. They are occasionally found overstruck by 6 nummi of Heraclius, so they do date before his reign.

A special class of 12 nummi appeared during the reign of Heraclius. This coin with its unique crowned facing bust surmounted by crescent and cross, has been attributed to the Persian king Khusru II and was struck by the Sasanians during their occupation of Egypt (618-628). In an inversion of the usual turn of events, these Persian copies (in two varieties) are larger than the Byzantine coins they supplant—the heaviest weighing 20 grams and more. Was Khusru merely attempting to impress the natives, or was his intention to circulate a bronze coin of equivalent value to the standard Persian silver drachm? Persian bronze coinage was rather sparse, while the Egyptians had

12 nummi of Khusru II, from Egypt

157

12 nummi of "Phocas" from Egypt. These types circulated widely in Palestine also

Imitation of a Constans II 12 nummi, from Egypt

Cast imitation of Heraclius, two bust type 12 nummi from Egypt, mintmark PAN

little experience with a circulating silver currency. The heavy 12 nummi may have been an attempt to meld two disparate systems. In any case, the Persian occupation of Egypt did not last long.

The remaining decades of the 7th century saw complete chaos in Egyptian monetary affairs. Heraclius never established a stable official currency, and the shortfall was made up with a tremendous variety of 12 nummi copies of variable quality. The copying continued into the Islamic period, with imitations of the coins of Constans II's brief incursion into Egypt in 645 added to the mixture. The mintmark ALEX, for Alexandria, which held firm during the previous century of imitation, broke down into strange permutations. Some numismatists have striven to put place names to some of these variations (PAN, MABA, MAKA, OBN and others), and attributed them to mints such as Panopolis and even Mecca. Most likely, they were merely the work of inexperienced engravers unfamiliar with both Greek and the significance of the designs they were copying.

The "Arab-Byzantine" series

With this last category we arrive at a region and time period that incites strong opinions among historians and numismatists. At issue is a clash of cultures that changed the outlines of the classical world and that still reverberates in the modern world. The effect on the coinage of the region is no less complex. Basically, after decades of internal and external strife, the Byzantine empire in the span of little more than a decade lost most of the eastern half of its territory to a new "superpower", the Muslim Arabs, that had little in common with its predecessor. One outcome of this clash was the complete overthrow of a coinage tradition that had lasted for centuries and its replacement with a new conception of coin design and function. It is the transitional series that interest us here.

Very briefly, the traditional view has defined "Arab-Byzantine" coinage as that coinage struck in Syria, Palestine and Egypt between

158

the Arab defeat of Byzantine forces and the death of Heraclius in 641 and the reform coinage of Abd al Malik struck beginning 695 featuring purely Islamic types. This coinage consisted of imitative folles of Byzantine type, some anonymous, some with the names of eastern cities, with a few extremely rare solidi added to the mix. Others have seen a more narrow focus of activity, with surviving Byzantine coinage circulating in the newly conquered lands until much later in the 7th century. At that time, they suggest, the Umayyad reforms responded to a coin shortage that prompted a brief period of "necessity coinage" lasting only a decade or so.

The true picture is probably much more complex. The East had been in turmoil since the beginning of the century, with Heraclius overthrowing the hated Phocas, only to be faced with simultaneous invasions by Avar and Persian, their overwhelming defeats to be followed in swift course by the eruption of a newly revitalized force out of Arabia, the Muslims, who would within a century control most of the near east and north Africa. What all this meant for the peoples of Syria and Palestine was that after 610, except for brief periods of truce, they were essentially on their own, responsible in large part for their essential needs, particularly a functioning currency system. In this situation civic councils, church authorities and local merchants probably worked to fill a growing gap.

In broad terms, outlined by S. Qedar and others, we have first an immense quantity of anonymous imitative bronzes of Heraclius and Constans II. Some of these are quite good and are only identifiable by inconsistencies in date and style from official issues. An example is the bronze folles of Heraclius from "Antioch" which did not strike for him and in any case are die-linked with other pieces with mintmarks of Constantinople and Nicomedia. Others must surely be counted among the most wretched pieces of metal even to dare take the name of "coin". Coins were prepared with complete lack of concern for style or standardization, struck in innumerable variations on broken up bits of earlier coins (sometimes centuries earlier) or even on

Transitional imitation follis, imitation of Heraclius, Antioch mint, year 14. Heraclius closed the Antioch mint without striking coins; this obverse is die-linked with coins bearing a Constantinople mintmark

Transitional imitation follis, crude imitation of Constans II

Transitional imitation follis, struck on a cut down Byzantine follis, the standing emperor and m of the overstrike barely visible

pieces of scrap metal, from tableware, bowls and plates with the decoration still visible. They all seem to have had no problem finding acceptance.

Alongside these rude issues (the chronology cannot be precisely determined, however) we find more carefully prepared issues bearing the names of important civic centers in the Syria-Palestine area (see facing page). An interesting subset of this class is comprised of folles and occasional half-folles whose prototype was the issue with Justin II and his wife enthroned. Mint names have been identified from Scythopolis (Beth-Shan) and Gerash in Greek, while others remain as yet unidentified. Another type with *Beisan* in Arabic suggests this class continued into the Islamic period. These issues can probably be grouped with Heraclius types bearing Jerusalem and Neapolis(?) mintmarks as the initiatives of local civic and ecclesiastical authorities in response to coin shortages.

True Arab-Byzantine issues combine renderings of Byzantine types with legends in both Greek and Arabic. Almost every important city struck these folles, Emesa and Damascus in Syria, Tiberias and Jerusalem in Palestine being among the most commonly encountered. However, new types and mints are always being uncovered—such as recent pieces from Eilat/Aqaba. A standing or half length imperial figure is the normal obverse type, with M reverse. The latest type is more explicitly Islamic, featuring a standing caliph and transformed cross on steps. These caliph folles, along with the extremely rare solidi of similar types, were most likely struck in the decade prior to the true Islamic coinage introduced at the end of the century. Traditional tales state that Abd al Malik was responding to Justinian II's placement of a portrait of Christ on his solidi when he forbade the striking of coins with graven images. The prosaic reality is that we are seeing in his new coinage the maturing of a new national identity, replacing classical culture.

Autonomous half follis of Scythopolis, type of Justin II, ΣΚΥΘΟ around

Three figure / M (Heraclius) fals of Tiberias, with legends in Greek and Arabic

Standing Caliph / M fals, probably struck at Amman

Autonomous follis of Gerash, type of Justin II, ΓΕΡΑSA retrograde to left

Autonomous follis of uncertain mint, type of Justin II, "OINK" (Nicomedia) mint

Autonomous follis of Neapolis(?), type of Heraclius, N below M

Facing bust / m (Constans II) fals of Emesa, with legends in Greek and Arabic

Imitation of a class A
Anonymous follis
from Asia Minor

Imitation of a class B
Anonymous follis
from Asia Minor

Imitation of a class I
Anonymous follis
from Asia Minor

The coinage of the preceding decades is inadequately described as "Arab-Byzantine"; it should be termed Byzantine Transitional or, if you will, Byzantine Provincial—or even, if you wish to link it more firmly to a long tradition of autonomous coinage, as Romaion Provincial!

The parallels of imitative coins to Byzantine mint products, as a series, are particularly evident in the case of anonymous folles of the 10th and 11th centuries. Illustrated here are a few examples of imitations that may be compared to the various "classes" of folles as we now categorize them.

A brief note should be made of a later Byzantine-influenced series, that of the Turkoman dynasties of the 12th-13th centuries. Imitations of later Byzantine folles did circulate in Asia Minor at this period, and the Zengid and Artuqid dirhems took similar forms. W.F. Spengler and W.G. Sayles have written a series of books covering these coins in exhaustive detail.

Zengid dirhem of Nur al din
Mahmud, imitating a follis of
Constantine X

(Peter Lampinen is a widely experienced numismatist and archaeologist specializing in coins of the Late Roman and Early Medieval periods. He is presently writing the catalogue of coins recovered in the ongoing excavation at Caesarea Maritima.)

BIBLIOGRAPHY
Imitative Issues

Adams, Lawrence A. "Gold Coinage of the Lombard Kingdom", *SAN*, XIII:1, 1982, pp. 4-10.

Album, Stephen. "Islamic conquerors adapted local Byzantine coinage", *The Celator*, 02:04, April 1988, p. 1ff.

Amin Awad, Henri. "Seventh Century Arab Imitations of Alexandrian Dodecanummia", *ANSMN* 18, 1972, pp. 113-117.

Balog, Paul. "Poids monétaires en verre Byzantino-Arabes", *Revue belge de numismatique*, 104, 1958, pp. 127-137.

Basok, Alexander. "Imitations of 11th Century Byzantine Coins Found on the Taman Peninsula", *Journal of the Russian Numismatic Society*, 66, 1998; also in *The Celator*, 12:11, 1998, pp. 6-15.

Bates, Michael L. "The 'Arab-Byzantine' Bronze Coinage of Syria: An Innovation by 'Abd al-Malik", *A Colloquium in Memory of George Carpenter Miles (1904-1975)*, ANS, New York, 1976.

Bates, M. and F. Kovacs. "A hoard of large Byzantine and Arab-Byzantine coppers", *Numismatic Chronicle*, 1996, pp. 165-173.

Bedoukian, P.Z. *Armenian Coinage*, 1962.

Bernareggi, Ernesto. "L'imitazione della moneta d'orodi Bisanzio nell'Europa barbarica", *Atti del convegno di studi longobardi Udine-Cividale 1969*, Udine, 1970.

Boutin, S. *Collection N.K. [Nadia Kapamadji]-Monnaies des Empires de Byzance*. 2 Vols. Maastricht, 1983. (An extensive private collection of Byzantine coins, with a particularly strong representative selection of western pseudo-imperial, with some eastern issues. A few debatable identifications, but overall a good source of illustrative types.)

Brooks, E.W. "The Arabs in Asia Minor (641-750), from Arabic Sources", *Journal of Hellenic Studies* XVIII, 1898, pp. 182-208.

Cahen, Claude. *Pre-Ottoman Turkey*, New York, 1968.

Courtois, Christian. *Les Vandales et l'Afrique*, Paris , 1955.

Crusafont i Sabater, M. *El Sistema Monetario Visigoda: Cobre y Oro*, Barcelona, 1994. (A recent reference for Visigothic coins, the first to organize the newly discovered Visigothic bronze coinage.)

Dobbins, Ed. "Sasanian bronze coins minted in Alexandria", *The Celator*, 08:11, November 1994, pp. 16-20.

Dochev, K. *Moneti i Parichno Obrushenie v Turnovo XII-XIVv*, Turnovo, 1992. (In Bulgarian, of course, but if one can work through enough of the Cyrillic, the charts and plates are very useful for identifying Bulgarian imitation and royal trachea.)

continued ☛

Goodwin, Tony. "The 'Standing Caliph' coinage", *The Celator,* 12:07, July 1998, pp. 20ff.

Gordus, A.A. and D.M. Metcalf. "The alloy of the miliaresion and the question of reminting of Islamic silver", *Hamburger Beiträge zur Numismatik,* 24/26, 1954, pp. 379-394.

Goussous, N.G. *Umayyad Coinage of Bilad al Sham,* Amman, 1996. (Production quality lags behind western standards, the English prose can be baffling at times, but still a useful source for illustrations of numerous rare varieties of transitional coinage struck in the provinces of Syria, Palestine and Jordan.)

Grierson, P. *Byzantine Coins,* Berkeley, 1982. (The best one volume introduction to Byzantine coinage, with sections on anomalous AE of the 6th century, pseudo-imperial western issues, Arab-Byzantine, Bulgarian and Latin imitations.)

___."The silver coinage of the Lombards", *Archivio storico lombardo,* 1956, pp. 130-147.

Grierson, P. and M. Blackburn. *Medieval European Coinage,* Cambridge, 1986. (The first volume in this series covers the western successor states. An upcoming volume will discuss coins of southern Italy, many with Byzantine connections.)

Hahn, W. *Moneta Imperii Byzantini,* 3 Vols. , Vienna. 1973-81. In German. (Excellent coverage of pseudo-imperial and "MMI" issues. His X-series illustrates a number of eastern transitional types, with little discussion.)

Hendy, M. *Coinage and Money in the Byzantine Empire 1081-1261,* Washington D.C., 1969. (The first work to lay out Bulgarian and Latin imitative coinages in a systematic manner.)

Ilisch, L. *Sylloge Numorum Arabicorum: Tübingen. Palästina. Tübingen. 1993-.* (This continuing series will eventually offer examples of many of the transitional types from Syria, Palestine and Egypt.)

Israel Numismatic Journal. (Has published a number of important articles by S. Qedar, R. Milstein and others on "Arab-Byzantine" issues.)

Kraus, Ferdinand F. *Die Münzen Odovacars und des Ostgothenreiches in Italien,* Halle, 1928 (Forni reprint 1967).

Metcalf, D.M. *Coinage of the Crusades and the Latin Eas,.* 2nd edition, London, 1995. (Useful study of the early folles of Edessa and Antioch.)

___. *Coinage in South-Eastern Europe 820-1396,* London, 1979. (Not a catalogue, but research tool using hoard data and accounts of trade links to put Balkan coinage in its historical context. Occasionally will derive a different conclusion from data than that put forward by Hendy.)

Metcalf, D.M. "The Peter and Paul hoard: Bulgarian and Latin imitative trachea in the time of Ivan Asen II, *Num. Chronicle*, 1973, pp. 144-172.

___."Byzantinobulgarica: the Second Bulgarian Empire and the problem of 'Bulgarian Imitative' trachea before and after 1204", *Numismatic Circular* 81, 1973, pp. 418-21.

___. "Some Byzantine and Arab-Byzantine coins from Palestina Prima", *Israel numismatic journal*, 2:3-4, 1964, pp. 32-46.

Miles, George C. *"Byzantium and the Arabs: relations in Crete and the Aegean area"*, Dumbarton Oaks Papers *18, 1964, pp. 1-32.*

___. *The coinage of the Visigoths of Spain: Leovigild to Achila II,* ANS, New York, 1952.

Ratto. R. *Monnaies Byzantines et d'autres Pays Contemporaines.* Lugano. 1930. An important private collection, often cited in references, although many identifications have to be corrected.

Runciman, S. *A History of the First Bulgarian Empire,* London, 1930.

Schlumberger, G. *Numismatique de l'Orient Latin,* 2 vols. 1878, reprint 1954.

Spengler, W.F. and W.G. Sayles. *Turkoman Figural Bronze Coins and Their Iconography,* 3 Vols. Lodi, Wisconsin, 1992-.

Tomasini, Wallace J. *The Barbaric Tremissis in Spain and Southern France, Anastasius to Leovigild,* ANS NNM 152, New York, 1964. A comprehensive study of the Visigothic pseudo-imperial series.

Yourlukova, Iordanka. "Imitations barbares de monnaies de bronze byzantines do VIe siècle", *Byzantinoslavica*, pp. 83-87, Prague, 1969.

Walker, J. *A Catalogue of Arab-Byzantine and Post-Reform Ommayyad Coins,* London, 1956. The standard reference, a few errors and fanciful identifications, but still important.

Wittek, P. *The Rise of the Ottoman Empire,* London, 1938.

Wroth, W. *Catalogue of the Coins of the Vandals, Ostrogoths and Lombards and of the Empires of Thessalonica, Nicaea and Trebizond in the British Museum,* London, 1911, (1966 Argonaut reprint as *Western and Provincial Byzantine Coins in the British Museum*). Still an important reference, although outdated in places.

Masterpieces
of Romaion Coinage

The following section includes a group of enlarged photographs of various Romaion coins considered by the author to be exceptional specimens. The selection is not based on any particular criteria, but mainly on visual and emotional appeal. Where Greek coins exhibited masterful creation of ideal images, and Roman coins displayed remarkable verism and narrative interest, Romaion coins display a different cultural preference.

The watchword of images from this period is spiritualism. It is a mark of excellence within the art of this time that the viewer can sense a spirituality in the subject rather than simply a mirror of nature. One might compare this philosophy to Platonic thinking in that everything has essence. Even a rock has an essence, and the ability to portray the essence of a rock, or "rockness" requires a certain spirituality. Consequently, great "Byzantine" art is not necessarily a reflection of good draftsmanship or of such worldly measures as perspective, modelling, and dimension.

Having said this, it is still possible within this style of art for all of these things to exist. When they do, however, they must be subordinate to the purpose of the composition.

Masterpieces of Romaion Coinage

Justinian I, AD 527-565
AE 20 nummi, Rome mint

The influence of Rome is readily apparent in this extraordinary issue, which could more easily pass for a portrait of Constantine the Great than of Justinian. The stylized hair, large spiritualistic eyes and lifeless diadem serve to minimize the worldly aspects of the subject. On the other hand, the high relief and sculptural quality of the jaw, chin and cheekbones create a sense of depth that is unusual for this time. The bullish neck and stern set to the mouth lend an aura of power and stability. Even the folds of drapery are carefully layered to create a sense of depth and realism.

Few works of art from this period exhibit these qualities—certainly not many coins. The bold contrasts of the ephemeral and the natural world meld together in a most effective way. It is inescapable that the artist who engraved this die was a master of his trade. The only other media in which this sort of balance is typically displayed are those of ivory miniatures and cameo or intaglio gems. One might conclude that the celator who created this die also worked in one of those fields.

Masterpieces of Romaion Coinage

Justinian I, AD 539/40 (year 13)
AE 40 nummi, Constantinople mint
(Actual Size)

One of the more remarkable things about the coin illustrated here is that it is presented at actual size! At better than 20 grams in weight and 45mm in diameter, it is among the largest and most impressive of all coins in this series. Like the specimen from Rome illustrated on the preceding page, this coin portrays the Great emperor Justinian. But what a remarkable difference in the nature of presentation!

Here, the subject is portrayed in a flat plane that deemphasizes the natural aspects of the man portrayed. The cuirass and shield, for example, are abstracted to a series of lines with no depth whatsoever. They merge into the surface of the coin with neither foreground nor background. Justinian's neck is engraved in such low relief that it tends to vanish into the fields. There is not the slightest form of expression, certainly nothing that would equate to a stern countenance. The whole composition takes on a rather geometric form. Everything is in symmetry—intensely rigid. The globe is held in a hand that is frozen in space.

This is precisely what the artist was trying to achieve, and the measure of his success is clear. While completely unnatural, and much different in tenor than its counterpart from Rome, this perfectly designed and exquisitely struck coin is a masterpiece.

Masterpieces of Romaion Coinage

Maurice Tiberius, AD 582-602
AE 40 nummi, Antioch mint

The regalia of imperial office was a thing of wonderment in the Later Roman Empire and it is especially well represented in the consular busts on coinage. Here, the emperor Maurice Tiberius has given us a calling card which reminds us that he, above all things, is a Roman Consul and Emperor.

Maurice holds in his right hand the mappa (napkin) which was thrown into the Hippodrome to signify the start of public games. In his left hand he holds the eagle-tipped scepter that signifies his rank as commander of all the empire's forces. The jewelled consular trabea, draped around his neck and crossed in the front, is a symbol of the high office which was theoretically held jointly by two consuls and elected annually. This is a bit anachronistic as the emperor usually did not share the power, nor require confirmation, in the later empire. His pearled crown bears a jeweled centerpiece with trefoil ornament and is adorned with pendilia—symbols of the imperial rank—which hang from each side. All in all, it presents an imposing picture.

Masterpieces of Romaion Coinage

Constantine IV, AD 668-685
AE 40 nummi, Constantinople mint
(Actual Size)

To appreciate this coin fully, one needs only to look at the rest of the bronze coinage of the seventh century. On the whole, it may be called "interesting" or "enigmatic", perhaps even "unusual", but few would call the coinage of this period *impressive*. Ragged flans, heavy debasement, crude striking and wretched die engraving are the norm. The enigma here is how the mint managed to produce a nearly round coin of such large flan, with a strong single strike on both sides and a nearly complete legend. Judging from the average seventh century "coin on the street" one would say that it was a mission impossible.

Aside from giving us a nice military snapshot of the emperor—albeit a rather plump sovereign as opposed to a lean general—we have quite remarkable depictions of his two sons, Heraclius and Tiberius, on the reverse. Seldom do we get to see the whole, unadulterated figure of one of these princes—much less both of them at the same time.

The striking of this impressive specimen could have been a statistical probability (sooner or later a nice one has to pop up) or more romantically, we may attribute it to the careful attention of a mintmaster who took his work seriously. In either case we are fortunate that time and fate have preserved this wonderful specimen for us.

Masterpieces of Romaion Coinage

Constantine VI and Irene, AD 780-797
AV solidus, Constantinople mint

The depiction of Irene wearing a loros and holding a globus cruciger reveals the extent of power wielded by this regent mother. It may be stretching the imagination a bit to say that this portrait is "delicate", but in contrast to other portrayals of the day it does call on one's emotions. Of course the real Irene was not at all a delicate person. Her ambition knew no bounds and she eventually gained the throne in her own name by deposing and blinding her own son. By this maneuver, she became the first woman to be enthroned at Constantinople as an independent sovereign.

Although Irene preferred to be called Basileus rather than Basilissa, she still wore the pointed crown of feminine nobility. In many ways she was more masculine than many who sat on the throne before her. She was not lacking in self-esteem—as this coin attests. The reverse is a carbon copy of the obverse. No, not a brockage, it is an intentional die-struck image of identical design.

Irene was not as adept at managing imperial affairs as she was at manipulating those around her. After a five year reign of increasing inefficiency and mounting pressure on the frontiers, Irene was deposed by a palace revolution and exiled to the island of Lesbos.

Masterpieces of Romaion Coinage

Leo V the Armenian, AD 813-820
AR miliaresion, Constantinople mint

This silver miliaresion of Leo V is the ultimate in simplicity—only a cross potent and a brief inscription. Yet, it embodies some extremely complex ideology. During this period, a bloody storm of controversy raged over the depiction of religious images. Those who rejected the use of icons believed that Christ was "uncircumscribable" and therefore not capable of being represented in the conception of an artist. The obverse of this coin, a straightforward portrayal of the Orthodox cross, reflects the will of Leo to restore the iconoclasm which his immediate predecessors chose not to enforce. In spite of his generally effective rule, this renewed prohibition of icons caused great civil unrest and proved to be Leo's undoing. He was assassinated by a group of religious zealots before the high altar at Hagia Sophia on Christmas day of 820.

The reverse legend of this coin proclaims Leo and his son Constantine as co-emperors of the Romans—"Basilis Romaion". A thorough discussion of the title may be found on pages 30-32. A discussion of Iconoclasm may be found on pages 26-27. In addition to being perfectly designed and struck, the state of preservation of this specimen is remarkable.

Masterpieces of Romaion Coinage

Leo VI & Constantine VII, AD 886-912
AV solidus, Constantinople mint

The opulence and splendor of Constantinople was broadcast to the world through the pomp of the imperial image. Every garment, symbol and gesture held a very precise and solemn meaning. Leo VI and his son Constantine VII are represented here as co-emperors. The inscription refers to them as "Leo and Constantine, Emperors of the Romans". The fact that Leo is senior emperor is made clear by their relative sizes, and by the fact that Leo stands on his own right.

The emperors are dressed in the divitision and loros, alluding to their role as vicars of Christ on earth. Between them they jointly hold a Patriarchal cross (with two cross arms) which symbolizes their unity with the church—at least outwardly. In their hands, each holds a globe with cross above (the globus cruciger). This device is a symbol of Christ as ruler of the universe.

The care with which this die was engraved is exceptional. The composition is balanced with perfect symmetry and the inscription is carefully placed and executed.

Masterpieces of Romaion Coinage

Alexander, AD 912-913, AV solidus
Constantinople mint

The scene on this coin is the first depiction of "heavenly investiture" on a Romaion coin. Here, Alexander is crowned by Saint Alexander—his patron saint. The legend, in Latin, refers to Alexander as "Augustus". Later, investiture scenes of this nature include those made by Christ, the Virgin, and a number of other saints. The *Manus Dei* (hand of God) appears on coins of an earlier time, dating back to the reign of Constantine the Great. This convention, where the hand generally extends down from the heavens, suggests the blessing of imperial rule but does not physically depict a coronation as in the scene here.

It is interesting that the cross held here by Saint Alexander is not the Patriarchal cross that we observed in the previous discussion, but the standard "Latin" cross with a single cross arm. This may be an intentional shift in iconography to avoid leaving the impression that the figure crowning the emperor is actually a depiction of the Patriarch. Although the specimen illustrated here suffers somewhat from normal wear, it is easy to see that the detail of the composition is quite similar to that of the coin struck earlier for Leo VI and Constantine (page 173).

Masterpieces of Romaion Coinage

Anonymous Follis, AD 976-1025
Constantinople mint

Anonymous folles are so called because they do not bear the name of any ruling authority. There are some fourteen varieties of this coinage, which have been identified by various numismatists according to "class". The particular class illustrated here, class A2, is the largest in size and perhaps the most impressive iconographically. It is generally accepted that this variety was issued during the reign of Basil II. The reverse of this type, and all others which bear legends, contains the phrase "Jesus Christ King of Kings" or some variant.

The obverse depiction of Christ is a famous and extremely popular icon of Christ Pantocrator. That is, Christ the ruler of the universe. The formula is one often seen on painted icons, mosaics, painted glass, incised metalwork, coins and virtually anything else that an image may be applied to. (For more about the Pantocrator motif see page 28.)

Masterpieces of Romaion Coinage

Romanus III, AD 1028-1034
AR miliaresion, Constantinople mint

This remarkable composition of the Virgin and Christ child was derived from a famous icon known as the "Virgin Hodegetria". It was said to have been painted by Saint Luke and was housed in the Hodegon monastery at Constantinople. The painting was supposedly found in Jerusalem by Eudocia, the wife of Theodosius II, about AD 443 and sent back to Constantinople. Hodegetria means literally, "showing the way". It refers to the nature of Mary as an interlocutor between God and man, and the theme is reflected in works from nearly every art medium. During time of distress, the Hodegetria icon was paraded through the streets of Constantinople to protect the city.

The coin's legend is an invocation for the intercession of Mary on the empire's behalf. In translation it reads "He who places his hope in thee, all-glorious Virgin, is successful in all he does". Romanus III was especially devoted to the veneration of the Virgin and built the church of St. Mary Peribleptos in her honor.

[See: Fagerlie, Joan M. "A miliaresion of Romanus III and a nomisma of Michael IV", *Museum Notes* 11, 1964, pp. 227-236.]

Masterpieces of Romaion Coinage

Michael VI, AD 1056-1057, AV tetarteron
Constantinople mint

Just as the Pantocrator became a familiar image in the post iconoclastic period, so too did the depiction of the Virgin Mary in the *Orans* posture. That is, with her hands raised in welcome. The role of Mary as intercessor was a key element in the Cult of the Virgin. Similar depictions in which the Virgin holds a medallion of Christ [an icon!] are called *Blacherniotissa*, in reference to a famous icon in the Blachernae monastery (see page 179).

The letters MP–ΘY which appear to the left and right of the Virgin's head are an abbreviation for *Μητηρ Θεον* or "Mother of God". This accolade was objected to by some early theologians who preferred the title *Ηαγια Μαρια*, or "Holy Mary" emphasizing her humanity as opposed to her divinity. By this period, the former had become standard phraseology and is found on virtually all coins bearing images of the Virgin.

Subtle treatments on this die, like the positioning of the hands, create deep impressions. It is interesting to compare, for example, the treatment of hands on the follis of Justinian I (page 168). As in all masterpieces of Romaion art, this composition radiates emotion through simplicity.

Masterpieces of Romaion Coinage

Michael VI, AD 1056-1057
AV histamenon nomisma, Constantinople mint

Rarely in this field of numismatics do we find coins that are well struck. Even more rarely, do we find them struck on large full flans. Finding a coin that is both is exceptional. Add to that an issue of great rarity and you have the makings of a masterpiece.

Michael Bringas, called Stratioticus, ruled for a very short time and issued few coins. His gold issues are very rare and the one silver issue is known from a unique coin. He did not issue any bronze coins that we know of. Fortunately, the surviving specimens in gold are generally well preserved. The specimen illustrated here is one of the great rarities of the series—in terms of quantity and quality.

If it is possible to think of coins from this era in terms of portraiture, this is a portrait coin. It not only presents an expressive (for the time) portrait of Christ on its obverse, but the reverse includes interesting portraits of the emperor and the Virgin who crowns him in the name of Christ. The macrocephalic figures might actually be recognized, had the engraver any sense at all of facial rendering. Of course, it was not in vogue to do so—at least not in the medium of numismatic art.

Masterpieces of Romaion Coinage

Romanus IV, AD 1068-1071
AV tetarteron, Constantinople mint

This particular depiction of the Virgin *Nikopoia* (holding medallion of Christ) is notable in that it emphasizes Mary's earthly role as mother—veiled but without the prominent nimbus that we have come to expect. This is a rare composition as such. It could be argued that this is a celator's error, and that the nimbus was simply forgotten, but there are earlier precedents (see the solidus of Leo VI, Sear 1723). The philosophical and dogmatic arguments of the day might account for a purposeful deviation from the standard nimbate Virgin.

The Third Ecumenical Council at Ephesus (AD 431) established the nature of Mary as *Theotokos*, "Godbearer". But controversy arose immediately over the term as Eastern Christians could not accept the argument that Mary's delivery was of God in a singular sense and not of a human. The resulting schism has lasted to this day. As emperors and Patriarchs changed in Constantinople, the nuances of religious reference changed as well—depending on their origins and beliefs. There are, of course, many dies of this coin type and the type itself was used by several emperors. Most others bear the Virgin's image nimbate. It is therefore unlikely that this specimen represents any official position on the subject. If it was an intentional omission of the nimbus, it was probably inspired by someone of strong beliefs and limited influence.

Masterpieces of Romaion Coinage

Theodore I Comnenus-Lascaris, AD 1208-1222
AR trachy, Magnesia mint

This coin tells us a great deal about the empire in exile at Nicaea. The drawn swords portray Theodore as a man of action in a time of crisis. The elaborate imperial dress suggests that he has not abandoned the traditions and dignity of the Romaion culture.

The figures on the reverse of this silver trachy are Theodore Lascaris and his patron saint Theodore. They stand side by side, both grasping an ornate labarum with stylized Chi-Rho symbol. The emperor stands on the left, which is his own right or the traditional place of honor. This symbol of rank has found its way down to the present time as ranking military members still walk on the right. The basis for this stems from the need to draw a sword cleanly. The scabbard is normally worn on the left, so that the sword is drawn with the right hand. The presence of a person to the right encumbers the movement of that drawn sword. Even saints have to stay out of the way of swords!

The workmanship of this die, and the two following masterpieces, makes it clear that trained and talented celators were available in spite of the provincial location. One might assume that when the patrons left Constantinople the artists left with them.

Masterpieces of Romaion Coinage

John III, Ducas-Vatatzes, AD 1222-1254
AE tetarteron, Magnesia mint

Where the follis of Justinian I shown earlier in this section (page 168) was notable for its massive size, this diminutive bronze is equally remarkable for its size and iconography. These tetartera typically measured about 18mm in diameter. The subject is Saint George, a legendary warrior and martyr, depicted with his shield and spear. Saint George was born in Asia Minor and was regarded as a champion of the faith—especially the Orthodox faith.

At a time when the empire was in very dire straits, and coinage in general was crude and poorly struck, this remarkable type stands out like a jewel. In fact, it is part of a series of jewels (see following page). The effort of John Vatatzes to rebuild the cultural infrastructure of his society is manifested not only in the public works and churches that he constructed, but in his patronage of artists and artisans. The entire series of coins from Nicaea reflects attention to the nature of images on coins—as if the emperors in exile used coinage to broadcast their pride and determination to survive.

Not all coins from Nicaea are as well centered and as well struck as the specimen illustrated here, but the designs that were engraved into dies were as good or better than anything that had been issued earlier at Constantinople.

Masterpieces of Romaion Coinage

— x1.5 —

Theodore II, Ducas-Vatatzes, AD 1254-1258
AE tetarteron, Magnesia mint

The sculptural quality of the coin discussed on the preceding page is evident as well on this small bronze tetarteron issued by John's son, Theodore II. The motif is simple, a device which has come to be known as the *Fleur-de-lis* (lily). Although this was a symbol of Charlemagne and the Frankish monarchy, it was also an attribute of the archangel Gabriel—a more likely reference in this case. Gabriel is said to have appeared before Mary at the Annunciation holding a lily in his hand. The most likely significance of the motif is provided by Grierson, who states that the fleur-de-lis is an attribute of Saint Tryphon, a local 3rd-century martyr whose relics annually caused the miracle of a lily blooming out of season on his feast day (February 1). The meaning of the four dots is unexplained. They may refer to something of religious significance, like the four evangelists, or they may be a mark of value. Another enigmatic motif of this reign has a composition including a large and ornate letter "B" with two clusters of three dots on each side. Again, the beauty of this unimposing coin is in its simplicity.

Additional References
Glossary
Index

Throughout this volume, we have included bibliographies wherever they might be helpful. These have been specific references to literature or catalogues which pertain to the topic under consideration. There are thousands of books and articles which include information of a more general nature. These can help us to understand the Romaion people and the climate in which they lived.

It was not possible to examine every book in the following lists and we cannot vouch for the accuracy or value of information which any particular one might contain. The lists were assembled from several sources, including: the recommendations of other authors; works in our own library which have been helpful; footnoted sources in texts which we have consulted; and from posting on the internet. It is, however, a selected bibliography in the sense that we did not include works that we felt might be unobtainable or difficult to translate. We have tried to disregard foreign language articles and books other than French and German, which are less likely to pose a serious problem. Fortunately, in numismatics, it is often possible to extract useful information from an article that is totally beyond the ability of the reader to translate. Many of the references will undoubtedly require the assistance of an interlibrary loan department to obtain. Unfortunately, this is the only way to get access to much of the information that has been published. Some readers will probably find that the lists are too long, and include too many esoteric references. Others will marvel at the breadth of material available. The truth of the matter is that this represents only a tiny fraction of what has been written.

Following the bibliographies, we have added a glossary of terms that are peculiar to the Byzantine/Romaion coins or culture. Standard numismatic terms and abbreviations will be found in our earlier volumes.

Finally, the general index which follows has been tabulated manually to avoid repetitive entries of little significance. Therefore, it will reflect some subjectivity on the part of the author. We apologize for any omissions that may delay the readers access to desired information.

BIBLIOGRAPHY
The Primary Sources

Nearly all of the references cited throughout this volume are secondary sources. That is partly because this is not an analytical or interpretive essay, but merely a synthesis of information available to the collector. Furthermore, most collectors are not able to read the primary sources in their classical languages. We recognize, however, that some collectors might like to evaluate information extracted from coins by their own comparisons with the ancient literature. Therefore, the following select (and certainly incomplete) list of primary sources in modern language translations is offered for that purpose:

Akropolites, George. *Chronike Sungraphe,* German tr. *Die Chronik / Georgios Akropolites; ubersetzt un erlautert,* by Wilhelm Blum, Stuttgart, 1989. (covers AD 1203-1261.)

Agathias of Myrina. "Agathias on the Sassanians", English tr. by Averil Cameron, *Dumbarton Oaks Papers* 23-24 (1969-70), pp. 67-183. (partial translation of Agathias, covers AD 552-559).

Cantacuzenus, John. *Historiarum,* English tr. (partial) as *The History of John Cantacuzenus, Book IV, Text, Translation and Commentary,* Catholic University of America, 1975. (Covers AD 1320-1357.)

Chrysostom, John. *Epistolae,* tr. into French as *Oeuvres complètes de saint Jean Chrysostome,* by Jeannin, M. Arras, 1887.

Comnena, Anna. *The Alexiad,* English tr. by E.R.A. Sewter, Penguin, NY, 1969. (Covers AD 1069-1118.)

Doukas. *Historia Turco-Byzantina,* English tr. as *Decline and Fall of Byzantium to the Ottoman Turks,* by Harry J. Magoulias, Wayne State Univ., 1975.

Eustathios of Thessalonica. "The Capture of Thessalonica", English tr. John Melville-Jones, *Byzantina Australiensia* 8, Canberra, 1988.

Evagrius. *Ecclesiastical History,* English tr. by E. Walford, Bohn's Ecclesiastical Library, London, 1854. (A continuation of the Ecclesiastical History of Eusebius covering the period 431-593.)

Indicopleustes, Cosmas. *The Christian Topography,* English tr. by J.W. McCrindle, Hakluyt Society Publications 98, London, 1897. (On commercial and economic life in the early 6th century.)

John of Ephesus. *Ecclesiastical History* (Part III only), English tr. by R. Payne Smith, Oxford, 1860. (Covers the years 521-585.)

Leo the Deacon. *Nikephoros Phokas 'Der bleiche Tod der Sarazenen' und Johannes Tzimiskes: die Zeit von 959 bis 976 in der Darstellung des Leon Diakonos,* tr. by Franz Loretto, Graz, Styria, 1961.

Malalas, John. *Chronographia,* English tr. of books VIII-XVIII by M. Spinka and G. Downey, Univ. of Chicago, 1940. (Chronicle of events to AD 563.)

Menander Protector. "The History of Menander the Guardsman", English tr. by R.C. Blockley, Liverpool: Francis Cairns, 1985. (covers AD 557-582)

Nicephorus Bryennios. *The Deeds of John and Manuel Comnenus,* English tr., Columbia University, 1976.

Nikephoros, Patriarch. "Short history / Nikephoros, Patriarch of Constantinople; text, translation and commentary", *Corpus fontium historiae Byzantinae,* v. 13, by Cyril Mango, Dumbarton Oaks, 1990. (cover s AD 602-769.)

Niketas Choniates. *Annals,* English tr. *O City of Byzantium, Annals of Niketas Choniates,* by Harry J. Magoulias, Wayne State Univ., 1984.

Nikiou, John of. *Chronicle,* English tr. by R.H. Charles, Text and Translation Society, London, 1916. (Translation of an Ethiopic version of an Arab copy of the lost Coptic original. Covers the period through the Arab conquest of Egypt.)

Pachymeres, George. *De Michaele et Andronico Paleologus,* French tr. of *Relationes historicas* by Vitalien Laurent, Paris: Less Belles Lettres, 1984.

Philotheos, *Kletorologion,* English text in The Imperial Administrative System in the Ninth Century, by J.B. Bury, London, 1911.

Procopius. *History of the Wars; Anékdota (Secret History); On the Buildings,* English tr. by H.B. Dewing, Loeb Classical Library, 1914-1940. (Covers the era of Justinian down to the mid 550s.)

Psellus, Michael. *Fourteen Byzantine Rulers, The Chronographia of Michael Psellus,* English tr. by E.R.A. Sewter, Penguin Books, New York, 1966. (Principal source for the Eastern Empire from AD 976 to 1078.)

Sebeos. *Hist. d'Héraclius,* translated to French by F. Macler, Paris, 1904.

Sphrantzes, *Chronicon Maius,* English tr. as *The Fall of the Byzantine Empire* by Marios Philippides, Univ. of Massachusetts Press, 1980.

Symeon the Logothere. *Chronicle,* English tr. as *The Chronicle of Symeon Logothetes,* publication pending.

Theophanes the Confessor. *Chronographia,* English tr. as *The Chronicle of Theophanes: An English Translation of anni muni 6095-6305 (A.D. 602-813)* by Harry Turtledove, Univ. of Pennsylvania, 1982.

Theophylakt of Simokatta. *The History of Theophylact of Simocatta: An English Translation with Introduction and Notes,* tr. by Michael and Mary Whitby, Oxford, 1986. (Covers the reign of Maurice Tiberius.)

BIBLIOGRAPHY
Romaion / Byzantine Coinage

Adelson, Howard L. "Silver currency and values in the early Byzantine empire", *Centennial publication of the American Numismatic Society*, New York, 1958, pp. 1-26.

___. *Light Weight Solidi and Byzantine Trade during the Sixth and Seventh Centuries*, ANS NNM 138, NY, 1957.

___. "A Note on the Miliarense from Constantine to Heraclius", *ANSMN VIII*, New York, 1957, pp. 125-135.

Bates, George E. *Sardis*, Vol. I, *Byzantine Coins, 1958-1968* (Archaeological excavation of Sardis), Harvard, 1971.

___. "A Byzantine hoard from Coelesyria", *ANSMN* 14, 1968, pp. 67-109.

___. "Three Byzantine Notes", *ANSMN* 14, 1968, pp. 111-120.

Bellinger, A.R. "Byzantine Notes", *ANSMN XII*, 1966, pp. 83-124. and *ANSMN* 13, 1967, pp. 123-166.

___. "The Coins and Byzantine Imperial Policy", *Speculum*, XXXI (1956), pp. 70-81.

___. *Catalogue of the Coins Found at Corinth, 1925*, New Haven, 1930.

Bellinger, Alfred, P. Grierson and M. Hendy *Catalogue of the Byzantine Coins in the Dumbarton Oaks Collection and in the Whittemore Collection*, Washington DC, 5 Vols. (incomplete), 1966-.

Bendall, Simon. "Rarities not expensive", *The Celator*, 03:09, September 1989, pp. 1 ff.

___. *A Private Collection of Palaeologan Coins*, Wolverhampton, 1988.

___. "Longuet's Salonica Hoard Reexamined", *ANSMN* 29, 1984, pp. 143-157.

___. *The Later Palaeologan Coinage*, London 1979 (with additions in *Numismatic Circular*, LXXXXVII 1979 and LXXXVIII, 1980).

___. "A Mid Seventh Century Hoard of Byzantine Folles", Numismatic Circular, 1967, pp. 198-201.

Berk, Harlan J. *Eastern Roman Successors of the Sestertius*, Chicago, N.D.

___. *Roman Gold Coins of the Medieval World, 383-1453 A.D.*, Joliet, 1986.

Bertelè, T. "Autocratori dei Romani, di Costantinopoli e della Macedonia", *Numismatica*, N.S. 2:2, 1961, pp. 75-82.

___. "Moneta bizantine inedite o rare", *Zeitschrift für Numismatik*, 36, (1926).

___. *Numismatique Byzantine*, ed. C. Morrisson, Wetteren, 1978.

Blake, Robert P. "The Monetary Reform of Anastasius I and its Economic Implications", *Studies in the History of Culture. The Disciplines of the Humanities*, Menasha, Wisconsin, 1942, pp. 84-95.

Boutin, S. *Collection NK, Monnaies des Empires de Byzance,* Maastricht, 1978 (collection of Nadia Kapamadji).

Briggs, David G. "New Byzantine Mint Issue Discovered", *The Numismatist,* May 1962.

Charanis, P. "The Significance of Coins as Evidence for the History of Athens and Corinth in the Seventh and Eighth Centuries", *Historia* IV, 1955, pp. 163-172.

Cheynet, J., C. Morrisson and W. Seibt. *Sceaux Byzantins de la Collection Henri Seyrig,* Paris, 1991.

Clark, Daniel C. *Speedy Identification of Early Denominationally Marked Byzantine Bronzes,* Tehachapi, CA, 1990.

Cutler, Anthony. "The stavraton: evidence for an elusive Byzantine type", *ANSMN* 11, 1964, pp. 237-244.

Fagerlie, Joan M. " 'Roma Invicta'—A New Follis of Justinian I", *ANSMN* XII, 1966, pp. 79-81.

Ferguson, Kevin. "Quantum Leap in Constantinople", *The Celator,* 12:01, January 1998, pp. 34-35.

Fox, Clifton. "What, if anything, is a Byzantine?", *The Celator,* 10:03, March 1996, pp. 36ff.

Goodacre, Hugh. *A Handbook of the Coinage of the Byzantine Empire,* London, 1964 (reprint).

Goodwin, Tony. "Byzantine coins provide opportunities for discovery", *The Celator,* 03:12, December 1989, pp. 20ff.

Grierson, P. *Byzantine Coins,* Berkeley, 1982.

___. "From solidus to hyperperon: the names of Byzantine gold coins", *The numismatic circular,* 74:5, 1966, pp. 123-124.

___. " The Tablettes Albertini and the value of the solidus in the fifth and sixth centuries A.D.", *Journal of Roman Studies* 49, pp. 73-80, 1959, London.

___. "The debasement of the nomisma in the 11th century", *Congrés international de numismatique, Vol. 2, Paris, 1953,* Paris, 1957.

___. "The debasement of the bezant in the eleventh century", *Byzantinische Zeitschrift,* 47, 1954, pp. 379-394.

Hahn, W. *Moneta Imperii Byzantini,* 3 vols., Vienna, 1973-1981.

___. "Alexandrian 3-nummi and 1-nummus types under Heraclius", *Numismatic Chronicle,* 138, 1978, pp. 181-183.

Hahn, W. and W.E. Metcalf. *Studies in Early Byzantine Gold Coinage,* ANSNS 17, New York, 1988.

Hammarberg, I., Brita Malmer and Torun Zachrisson. *Byzantine Coins Found in Sweden,* Spink, London, 1989.

Hendy, M.F. *Studies in the Byzantine Monetary Economy c. 300-1450,* Cambridge, 1985.

☞

___. "The tetarteron in the twelfth century", *Numismatic Circular* 86, 1978, p. 574.

___. "Light weight solidi, tetartera and the Book of the Prefect", *Byzantinische Zeitschrift*, 65, 1972, pp. 57-80.

___. "Byzantium 1081-1204: an economic reappraisal", *Transactions of the Royal Historical Society*, 1970, pp. 31-52.

___. "On the administrative basis of the Byzantine coinage ca. 400-ca. 900 and the reforms of Heraclius", *Historical Journal* 12:2, University of Birmingham, 1970, pp. 129-154.

___. *Coinage and Money in the Byzantine Empire, 1081-1261*, Dumbarton Oaks Studies XII, Washington, 1969.

Hendy, M.F. and J.A. Charles. "The production techniques, silver content and circulation history of the twelfth century Byzantine trachy", *Archaeometry*, 12, 1970, pp. 13-21.

Herrin, Judith. "The collapse of the Byzantine Empire in the twelfth century" a study of medieval economy", *Historical Journal*, 12:2, 1970 (University of Birmingham), pp. 188-203.

Kent, John. *A Selection of Byzantine Coins in the Barber Institute of Fine Arts*, Birmingham, 1985.

Kroh, Dennis J. "Books on the coinage of the Byzantine empire", *The Celator*, 05:04, April 1991, p. 36ff.

Lacam, Guy. *Civilisation et monnaies byzantines*, Paris, 1974.

Laurent, V. "Bulletin de Numismatique Byzantine, 1940-1949", a bibliography in *Revue des Etudes Byzantines*, vol. 9, 1951.

Lhotka, J.F., Jr. *Introduction to East Roman Coinage*, 1954 (Durst reprint)

Longuet, H. *Introduction à la Numismatique byzantine*, London, 1961.

___. "Un Trouvaille de Monnaies des Palaeologues", *Revue Belge Numismatique*, 1960, pp. 243-66.

___. "Die unedierten byzantinischen Münzen des Wiener Kabinettes", *Numismatische Zeitschrift, 1957*.

Lopez, R.S. "The Dollar of the Middle Ages", *Journal of Economic History*, XI, 1951, pp. 209-234.

Malter, Joel. *Byzantine Numismatic Bibliography, 1950-1965*, Chicago, 1968.

___. "Byzantine hoards, finds and excavation coins, 1950-1965", *North American Journal of Numismatics*, 07:04, 1968, pp. 122-125.

Metcalf, D.M. *Coinage in south-eastern Europe 820-1396*, Royal Numismatic Society, Special Publication 11, London, 1979.

___. *Classification of Byzantine Stamena in the Light of a Hoard found in Southern Serbia*, Ljublana, 1967.

___. "The Aegean coastline under threat: some coins and coin hoards from the reign of Heraclius", *Annual of the British School of Archaeology at Athens*, LVII, 1962, pp. 14-23.

___. "Provincial issues among the Byzantine bronze coinage of the eleventh century", *Hamburger Beiträge zur Numismatik*, 5:15, 1961, pp. 25-32.

Miles, George. "Byzantine miliaresion and Arab dirhem; some notes on their relationship", *Museum Notes* 9, 1960, pp. 189-218.

Morrisson, C. *Catalogue des Monnaies Byzantines de la Bibliothéque Nationale.* 2 vols., Paris, 1970.

Mosser, Sawyer McA, *Bibliography of Byzantine Coin Hoards*, ANS NNM 67, NY, 1935.

Newell, Edward T. *The Byzantine Hoard of Lagbe*, ANS NNM 105, NY, 1945.

Ratto, R. *Monnaies Byzantines et d'autres Pays Contemporaines*, Lugano, 1930 (1959 Hans Schulman reprint).

Reding, Frederick P. "New varieties of Byzantine coins", *The Celator*, 07:11, November 1993, p.16ff.

Ricotti-Prina, D. *La Monetazione Aurea delle Zecche Minore Bizantine dal VI al IX Secolo*, Rome, 1972.

Rynearson, Paul F. *Byzantine coin values: A guide*, San Diego, 1967.

Sabatier, J. *Description Generale des Monnaies Byzantines*, 2 vols., Paris, 1863 (1955 Graz, Austria, reprint).

Saulcy, F. de. *Essai de classification des suites monétaires byzantines*, Paris, 1836.

Sear, David. *Byzantine Coins and Their Values*, 2nd. Ed., London, 1987.

Sotheby's. *The William Herbert Hunt Collection of Highly Important Byzantine Coins*, (Dec. 5-6, 1990) and *Important Byzantine Coins*, (June 21, 1991), New York.

Spaer, A. "The Rafah Hoard. Byzantine Sixth-Century Folles", *Numismatic Chronicle*, 1978, pp. 66-70.

Stein, E. "Post-consulat et AYTOKPATOPIA", *Mélange Bidez, Annuaire d l'Institut de Philologie et d'Histoire Orientales*, II, 1934, pp. 887ff.

Tolstoi, Count Ivan. *Vizantiiskia Monety*, St. Petersburg, 1912-1914. also as *Monnais Byzantines*, Amsterdam, 1968 (Hakkert reprint).

Vryonis, Speros. "An Attic hoard of Byzantine gold coins (668-741) from the Thomas Whittemore collection and the numismatic evidence for the urban history of Byzantium", *Mélanges Georges Ostrogorsky I*, Belgrade, 1963, pp. 291-300.

Whitting, P.D. *Byzantine Coins*, New York, 1973.

Wroth, W. *Catalogue of the Imperial Byzantine Coins in the British Museum*, 1908, (1966 Argonaut reprint).

Zakythinos, D.A. *Crise monétaire et crise économique à Byzance du XIII au XVe siècle*, Athens, 1948.

BIBLIOGRAPHY
Romaion/Byzantine Art

Ainalov, D.V., tr. by E. & S. Sobolevitch. *The Hellenistic Origins of Byzantine Art,* Rutgers, 1961.

Beckwith, J. *Art of Constantinople,* London, 1961.

Bellinger, A.R. "Roman and Byzantine Medallions in the Dumbarton Oaks Collection", *Dumbarton Oaks Papers,* 12 (1958).

Bendall, Simon. *Byzantine Weights: An Introduction,* London, 1996.

Bevan, E. *Holy Images,* London, 1940.

Dalton, O. *Byzantine Art and Archaeology,* Oxford, 1911.

Delvoye, Charles. *L'art byzantin,* Paris, 1967.

Didron, A.N. *Christian Iconography, The History of Christian Art in the Middle Ages,* 1st ed. 1851, tr. E.J. Millington, reprints, New York, 1965 & 1968.

Frolow, A. "Les noms de monnaies dans le Typicon du Pantocrator", *Byzantinoslavica,* 10, 1949, pp. 241-253.

Galavaris, George P. "The symbolism of the imperial costume as displayed on Byzantine coins", *ANSMN* 8, 1958, pp. 99-117.

Grabar, A. *Byzantium. From the Death of Theodosius to the Rise of Islam,* London, 1966.

___. *L'iconoclasme byzantin. Dossier archéologique,* Paris, 1957.

___. *L'empereur dans l'art Byzantin,* Strasbourg, 1936 (1971 reprint).

Grierson, Philip. "Byzantine gold bullae, with a catalogue of those at Dumbarton Oaks", *Dumbarton Oaks Papers* 20, 1966, pp. 239-253.

___. "The Kyrenia Girdle of Byzantine Medallions and Solidi", *Numismatic Chronicle,* 1955, p. 67ff.

Kitzinger, E. "Some reflections on portraiture in Byzantine art", *Mélanges Georges Ostrogorsky I,* Belgrade, 1963.

MacCormack, S. G. *Art and Ceremony in Late Antiquity,* Berkeley, 1981.

Martin, E.J. *A History of the Iconoclastic Controversy,* London, 1930.

Oikonomides, N. *Byzantine Lead Seals,* Dumbarton Oaks, Byzantine Collection Publications No. 7, Washington, 1985.

Rice, D. Talbot. *Art of Byzantium,* London, 1959.

Sayles, Wayne G. "Spiritualism of later Roman art became the hallmark of Byzantine style", *The Celator,* 05:01, January 1991, p. 40ff.

Voirol, A. "Die ersten Darstellungen von Christus und von Maria auf byzantinischen Münzen", *Schweizer Münzblätter,* 32, 1958, pp. 113-17.

Whitting, P.D. "Iconoclasm and the Byzantine coinage", *Historical Journal* 12:2, (Univ. of Birmingham), pp. 158-163, 1970.

Zacos, G. and A. Veglery. *Byzantine Lead Seals,* 2 vols., Basel, 1972-1984.

BIBLIOGRAPHY
General History

Baynes, N.H. *The Hellenistic Civilization and East Rome,* Oxford, 1946.
___. *The Byzantine Empire,* Oxford, 1943.
Baynes, N.H. and H. Moss, *Byzantium: An Introduction to East Roman Civilization,* Oxford, 1962.
Brown, Peter. *The World of Late Antiquity, AD 150-750,* London, 1971.
Bury, J.B. *A History of the Later Roman Empire from the Death of Theodosius I to the Death of Justinian,* 2 vols., London, 1923.
___. *A History of the Later Roman Empire from Arcadius to Irene (395-800),* 2 vols. 1889.
___. *A History of the Eastern Roman Empire from the Fall of Irene to the Accession of Basil I (802-807),* London, 1912.
Cambridge Medieval History, 2nd ed. vols. , 1913, revised 1926.
Diehl, C. *Byzantium: Greatness and Decline,* tr. by N. Walford, Rutgers, 1957.
___. *Byzantine Portraits,* tr. by H. Bell, New York, 1927.
___. *Justinien et la civilisation byzantine au VIe siécle,* Paris, 1901, (reprint New York, 1959).
Downey, G. *Constantinople in the Age of Justinian,* Oklahoma University Press, 1960.
Every, G. *The Byzantine Patriarchate, 451-1204,* London, 1962.
Gibbon, Edward. *Decline and Fall of the Roman Empire,* 1776 (many reprints and editions).
Hussey, J. *The Byzantine World,* Hutchinson, 1961.
Jones, A.H.M. *The later Roman Empire, 284-602: A Social, Economic and Administrative Survey,* 4 vols., Oxford, 1964.
Kazhdan, A.P. and Ann Wharton Epstein. *Change in Byzantine Culture in the Eleventh and Twelfth Centuries,* Berkeley, 1985.
Kollgaard. Ron. "The Fall of Rome and the Early Byzantine Empire", *The Celator,* (in four parts, Dec. 1992 - Mar. 1993).
Lamb, Harold. *Constantinople: Birth of an Empire,* Robert Hale, 1958.
___. *Theodora and the Emperor,* Doubleday, 1952.
McManners, John. ed. *The Oxford Illustrated History of Christianity,* Oxford, 1990.
Nicol, Donald M. *A Biographical Dictionary of the Byzantine Empire,* London, 1991.
Norwich, John Julius. *Byzantium: A History,* Knopf, New York, 1997.
___. *The Last Centuries of Byzantium,* Rupert Hart Davis, 1972.

☞

Ostrogorsky, George. "The Byzantine Empire in the World of the Seventh Century", *Dumbarton Oaks Papers* XIII, 1959, pp. 1ff.

___. *History of the Byzantine State*, Rutgers, 1957.

Runciman, S. *History of the Crusades*, Cambridge, 1954.

___. *Byzantine Civilisation*, New York and London, 1933.

Sphrantzes, George. *The Fall of the Byzantine Empire*, tr. Marios Philippides, University of Massachusetts, 1980.

Stevenson, J. *Creeds, Councils and Controversies*, London, 1966.

Sullivan, Richard E. *Heirs of the Roman Empire*, Cornell, 1960.

Treadgold, Warren. *A History of the Byzantine State and Society*, Stanford, 1997.

Vacolopoulos, A.E. *Origins of the Greek Nation, the Byzantine Period, 1204-1461*, Rutgers, 1970.

Vasiliev, A.A. *History of the Byzantine Empire, 324-1453*, Univ. of Wisconsin, 1952.

Wilson, N.G. *From Byzantium to Italy: Greek Studies in the Italian Renaissance*, Johns Hopkins, 1992.

___. *Byzantium: An Introduction*, New York University, 1971.

Yannopoulis, P. *L'Exagramme. Un Monnayage Byzantin en Arrgent du VII siècle*, Louvain-la-Neuve, 1978.

Glossary

Agia: see Hagia

Anastasis: The Resurrection (also the feast of this day).

Akakia: Scroll-like object with knobs on the ends, took the place of the mappa as a symbol of imperial authority .

Archon: Governor.

Asper: Greek for "white", used to designate silver coins.

Aspron Trachy: The electrum (white gold) concave coin.

Autocrator: Imperial title.

Baldachin: Canopy with slender pillars used to enclose an altar.

Basileus: Greek for "king", an imperial title.

Basilicon: Small silver denomination introduced by Andronicus II.

Bezant: Western name for the solidus.

Bulgaroctonos: Slayer of the Bulgars (Basil II).

Chi Rho: Monogram consisting of the first two letters in the name Christ.

Chlamys: Purple mantle worn by the emperor, fastened at the right shoulder with a decorative cloth and pin. Imperial state costume.

Colobium: Short tunic worn as an undergarment.

Copts: Christians in Egypt

Deesis: Christ represented between the Virgin and John the Baptist.

Decanummium: bronze coin of 10 nummi.

Despot: Greek for "Lord" or "Master", an imperial title of lesser rank than Basileus.

Diadem: Imperial headband adorned with pearls or jewels.

Divitision: A long belted tunic with close fitting sleeves.

Dormition: Death of the Virgin.

Drungarius: Commander of a "drungus" or body of infantry.

Ecumenical: Meaning "open to all", as in councils of church leaders.

Eidikos: Master of the imperial wardrobe.

Emmanuel: Term given to depictions of the infant Christ.

Eparch: Equivalent of the Roman Praefect, a governor or chief official.

Globus Cruciger: Globe surmounted by a cross.

Hagia: Holy; Greek equivalent of "saint" in regard to a person.

Hexagram: Silver coin weighing six gramma = 1/4 of a Roman ounce.

Histamenon: Greek, meaning "standard" or full weight.

Hodegetria: "showing the way", title given the Virgin Mary.

Hyperpyron or hyperperon: Greek, meaning "highly refined".

Icon: Any image of a sacred person or scene.

Iconoclast: Destroyer of images.

Iconodule: Servant of images.

Indiction: Fifteen year cycle by which coins were dated.

Khan: Turkish title for "supreme leader".

Koimesis: see Dormition.

Labarum: The Christian standard bearing Chi-Rho symbol.

Logothete: Counsellor to the Basileus (in some cases treasurer).

Loros: A rectangular piece of cloth, or scarf, by which the emperor is symbolically projected as the visible representative of Christ. Derived from the Roman "trabea" worn by consuls.

Magister: Meaning "master", as in Magister Militum, master of the army.

Mandorla: The oval field of radiance surrounding a holy person.

Maphorion: Veil worn by the Virgin.

Mappa: roll of cloth (a napkin) tossed into the stadium to start the games.

Miliaresion or Miliarense: The standard silver coin to the 11th century.

Nimbate: With halo about the head.

Nomisma: Literally, "coin".

Nummus: The smallest copper coin and unit of accounting.

Obryzium: The term for pure gold (OB).

Orans: "Praying", as in representations of the Virgin with hands raised.

Paludamentum: Ceremonial military cloak of a Roman general.

Pammakaristos: Most blessed.

Pantocrator: "all sovereign" ruler, i.e., ruler of the universe.

Parazonium: An item worn on the belt.

Patriarch: The spiritual head of the Eastern church.

Patriarchal Cross: Cross with two sets of cross arms.

Pendilia: Pendants hanging from the sides of an imperial crown.

Pentanummium: Bronze coin of five nummi.

Peribleptos: Notable and admired.

Politikon: An urban or municipal reference, used on "city" coins.

Potent: Term used to describe a cross with a bar at the end of each arm.

Proskynesis: A practice originating in the East which entails falling on one's knees before the emperor (or representation of the emperor or Christ) and touching the ground with one's forehead with arms outstretched.

Sakkos: a long black undergarment symbolizing the mystery of the emperor.

Scyphate: A term used to describe cup-shaped coins.

Semissis: One-half solidus.

Siliqua: The Latin term for carat. 1/24th of a solidus of pure gold.

Stavraton: From "cross", a term applied to coins with the emperor holding a cruciform scepter, or with legends starting with a cross.

Stemma: Flat imperial crown.

Stemmatargyrion: Domed imperial crown.

Strategus: General or commander of a theme.

Tablion: A lapel-like piece of decorated cloth at the chest on the chlamys.

Tetarteron: Lightweight gold nomisma, also a bronze coin of similar size.

Theometor: Mother of God.

Theotokos: "Godbearer".

Toufa: Imperial diadem with crest of peacock feathers.

Trabea: Large purple cloth decorated with jewels, Greek "loros". Originally signified triumph, later divine authority to rule.

Trachy: Greek term for concave coins, also called scyphate.

Tremissis: One-third solidus.

Trilobate: Three lobed, as in a trilobate scepter.

General Index

☛

*For the index of
Emperors see
page 122*

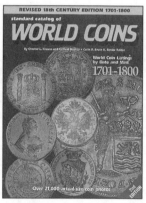
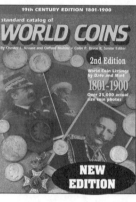